The Weather Business

Other Books in this Series

The Weather Business

Observation, Analysis, Forecasting, and Modification

Bruce W. Atkinson

Doubleday Science Series
Doubleday & Company, Inc.
Garden City, New York, 1969

THE WEATHER BUSINESS: Observation, Analysis, Forecasting, and Modification
was published simultaneously in a hardbound edition by Doubleday &
Company, Inc.
First published in the United States of America in 1969 by
Doubleday & Company, Inc., Garden City, New York,
in association with Aldus Books Limited.
Copyright © Aldus Books Limited, London, 1968
Printed in Italy by Arnoldo Mondadori, Verona

Contents

1 Weather and Man

Man is a weather-sensitive creature. Most of his activities, from industry to agriculture, from space research to sport, are directly influenced by a background of weather—at times dramatically, as in the Italian floods of 1966 or the annual hurricanes on America's eastern seaboard. The ways in which man himself unwittingly influences the weather are perhaps not so readily recognized, but there is a distinct feedback from his activities. His constant modification of the earth's surface, whether by clearing forests for farming or by building towns and cities, has led to small, localized changes in the characteristics of the lowest layers of the atmosphere. Most urban areas, for example, develop their own climates, which are quite different from those of the surrounding countryside. Temperature, pollution, cloudiness, and even rainfall tend to have increased values in the city. In addition, conscious attempts

Aftermath of a catastrophe. In November 1966 unusually heavy rains in northern Italy made the river Arno overflow its banks, killing 118 people, destroying the ancient Ponte Vecchio in Florence, and causing damage to property, including paintings and other art treasures, estimated at $1500 million. Extremes like this are rare, but even moderate changes in weather can have serious results.

have been made since World War II to modify weather in some areas, with, as yet, only a limited degree of success.

Despite the profound effects not only extremes but also normal day-to-day changes of weather have upon man, it is only comparatively recently that systematic observations of the behavior of the atmosphere have been carried out. There were some crude attempts at measuring rainfall about 2000 years ago; in the 17th century and later, observations of temperature and pressure were made by people for their own purposes: but the study of the atmosphere long remained a branch of physical science cultivated by a few keen amateurs who had the opportunity to satisfy their own interest. By the 19th century, however, it was appreciated that local studies of the atmosphere by isolated observers were of limited value to our understanding of the weather. The first moves toward an international approach were made in 1853, when a meeting of maritime nations drew up a program of weather observation over the oceans to achieve greater safety at sea. In 1878 the directors of the national weather services established the International Meteorological Organization (IMO) whose aim was the orderly observation of the weather. This cooperative effort developed steadily over the next 70 years, concentrating on the improvement of the services provided by meteorologists for navigation and agriculture, and the setting up of a system for exchanging weather information along air routes and at airfields. A tremendous impetus to the study of the weather resulted. After World War II the IMO was reconstituted as the World Meteorological Organization (WMO), and in December 1951 the United Nations recognized the WMO as a specialized agency.

The WMO exists to further the application of meteorology to aviation, shipping, agriculture, and many other human activities. This requires a worldwide exchange of meteorological information for forecasting and research, and more than 130 countries (see page 11) now collaborate to make this exchange a daily reality. In all these countries, the methods of weather observation, coding, and transmission are determined by the regulations of the WMO. We can see from the map that meteorology today is a science that recognizes few political frontiers.

The World Meteorological Organization (member countries in gray) was recognized by the United Nations as a specialized agency in 1951. It provides for the world-wide exchange of information for forecasting and research, and aims at applying weather technology to the practical requirements of aviation, shipping, agriculture, and other human activities.

In this book we shall look at some of the techniques used today to observe, analyze, forecast, and even modify the world's weather. We start with observation by the global network and then outline methods of analysis and forecasting. In all three stages—observation, analysis, and forecasting—the handbooks issued by the WMO are indispensable to the practicing meteorologist. Our rather haphazard attempts to modify the weather receive some consideration in Chapter 5. We conclude with a look into the future to examine in particular the global improvements taking place as part of World Weather Watch, the current three-year cooperative effort by members of WMO to solve a wide range of meteorological problems, which is due to end in 1971. First, however, let us look in a little more detail at the way we are affected by the weather and how weather services try to cater for our needs.

12

Man as an Individual

The influences of the atmospheric elements upon all biological phenomena are the province of biometeorology. Within this broad field, meteorologists and physiologists have studied many responses of the human body to atmospheric characteristics. The life, health, and comfort of a human being, as well as of most of the world's animal life, are heavily dependent on the range of values of temperature, humidity, wind speed, radiation, pressure, and aerosol content in the atmosphere. (*Aerosol* is the suspension of solid or liquid particles—usually about one micron in diameter—such as those that make up haze or smog.) At their extremes, with the one exception of humidity, all are capable of causing death, and the combined effect of less extreme values can often be detrimental to health and comfort.

Many attempts have been made to define the meteorological conditions that are limiting for men engaged in various activities. The most common method is to derive empirical relationships between human activity and certain atmospheric *parameters* or variables, such as dry bulb and/or wet bulb temperature. Although some of these indices have been modified by the addition of physiological parameters such as rate of heat production in the body, the simple relationship between meteorological element and human activity is still a useful guide, particularly in military planning. One example of the possible ranking of environmental conditions according to the

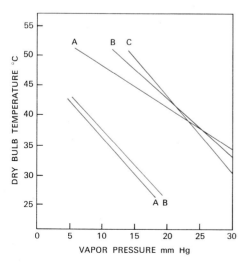

Graph showing safety limits of strains imposed by weather conditions on the human body. The blue lines represent limits for acclimatized man: line A describes conditions under which man can comfortably and safely do light work; line B separates very warm conditions (risk of heat stroke) from intolerably hot conditions (heat stroke likely); line C describes safe limit for employees in mines and textile mills. Red lines give limits for unacclimatized man: line A separates warm from very hot conditions; line B describes critical threshold to heat stroke for United States military personnel.

strains imposed on the thermoregulatory and circulatory systems is shown on page 12: it is important to note that the lines do not represent the upper limits of heat tolerance for human beings, but safe limits below which effective physical and mental work can be carried out for reasonably long periods of exposure. The obvious influence of extreme values of dry bulb temperature and humidity is well illustrated here.

The combined effects of *temperature, humidity*, and *air motion* are considered to be the most important meteorological elements that may influence the running efficiency of the human body. It has been known for some time that man is essentially a tropical animal. Experiments have shown that, unclothed and without shelter, he is adapted to a temperature of 20.4°C with moderate humidity and low air movement. To protect himself against lower temperatures his own heat production must increase, but, of course, there are limits to what is physiologically possible. Thus to accommodate a temperature of −1.0°C the total metabolism rate would have to be eight times its usual value, and this cannot be maintained over long periods. There is also an upper limit to what we might loosely call a comfortable environment. According to most authorities this is 26.1°C with a relative humidity of 75 per cent. Again, because one of the most important cooling agents for the body is the evaporation of sweat into the atmosphere, comfort is to a large extent dependent, too, upon humidity and wind speed.

The establishment of all such relationships is the basis of what may be called *medical-meteorological* forecasting. This predicts the reactions of men to extremes of weather, and is a vital consideration in military and other outdoor activities. As such it is not undertaken on a routine basis—as are the daily weather forecasts issued by most national meteorological services—but this does not reduce its importance.

The direct effects of *solar radiation* on man are of two kinds: the responses resulting from photochemical reactions, and those from body heating. The most common manifestation of the first is sunburn, which involves injury to the cells at the base of the living layer of skin and is caused by radiation in ultraviolet wavelengths shorter than about 0.32μ. The second effect results in an increase of body heat, which, in order to prevent body temperatures from rising dangerously, must be lost by conduction, convection, and evaporation of sweat. If the human body cannot get rid of its heat load, the result may be heat stroke.

The most significant effect of *pressure* on the human body is that of the marked decrease in the partial pressure of oxygen at high altitudes. This may result in respiratory difficulties, an increase in heart beat, and the alteration of blood composition. To offset these difficulties the human body acclimatizes itself to the upland environment by physiological adaptations; these concern all the body functions and enable man to survive and carry on quite vigorous activities at high altitudes. In the Andes there are permanent habitations at altitudes of about 5500 m. but these are extreme cases. The more important effects of moderately high altitudes have not been investigated as fully as we might wish. This became evident recently in the light of the decision to hold the 1968 Olympic Games in Mexico City at a height of 2500 m. Although the effects were small compared to those experienced at altitudes of 5000–6000 m., they had an effect on the athletes' performances. To a lesser extent, rapid fluctuations of pressure have direct effects on man. We are all familiar with "popping" sensations in our ears when we rapidly ascend or descend even quite small distances. On a larger scale there are authentic cases of pressure variations during ordinary weather changes causing an annoying amount of pain by, for example, aggravating old wounds.

Smog exerts heavy respiratory and circulatory stresses on the human body, stresses that may be so great as to cause death from cardiac failure in those already suffering from such ailments. It is fairly certain that in the London smog of December 1952, 4000 deaths were caused primarily by the high concentration of SO_2 and smoke in the atmosphere. Such drastic concentrations are fortunately rare, but this extreme example shows that the aerosol content of the air can, and does, markedly affect the health and comfort of many people. Its effects upon society will be dealt with later.

Weather and Agriculture

In its most extreme form, weather can destroy both man and his agricultural crops and animals. Similarly, just as human health and comfort are influenced by less extreme weather conditions, so is the productivity of crops and animals. Although only extreme influences are considered here, it is important to remember that, by patient research into the relationships between crops and animals and weather conditions, the efficiency of agriculture has been markedly increased.

Hazards in agriculture fall into two main classes—local and widespread. The first includes sudden floods, hail, lightning, tornadoes, and fire; the second includes widespread floods, drought, diseases and pests, gales, snow, and frost.

Sudden or flash floods are the result of heavy rain falling for a short period over a small area. The actual fall of rain in such a situation is often sufficient to ruin a crop by flattening it, but this is normally minor damage compared to the devastation of widespread flooding. Hail is similar in its erratic behavior and can damage buildings as well as flatten cereals and strip orchards. In some parts of the world, such as the southern states of the United States, hailstones may attain a diameter of 2.5 cm. or more, and consequently become very dangerous indeed: in Britain, they are rarely over 1.25 cm. in diameter. Lightning is often found in association with hail but, apart from the occasional direct strike on a human being, its effect is not as bad as might at first be supposed. Lightning may start fires in crops or in forests, however, and special forest-fire forecasting services have been set up in several countries, notably the United States and Australia. The combined effects of lightning, hail, rain, and high wind make the tornado perhaps the most destructive of all the atmospheric systems. Although its path is often quite narrow—sometimes only a few hundred meters wide—it may travel for tens of kilometers, and within its range devastation is usually complete. Not only are crops ruined and livestock lost, but whole farmsteads may disappear. The cost of the damage caused by tornadoes for one year in the United States alone can be as much as $200 million (1965).

Left: tornadoes like this one are perhaps the most destructive of all weather phenomena. In the United States, damage caused by tornadoes can cost as much as $200 million a year (1965). Right: excessive droughts, such as the one in Bihar, India, which started in 1965, can bring famine, disease, and death: one estimate put the number of deaths caused by this one at two million. Far right: a locust swarm in Israel. The mass movements of these insects are largely directed by patterns of airflow.

Tornadoes, together with all the other hazards noted above, have one thing in common; they are very difficult, if not impossible, to forecast. Fortunately they are limited in space and time, and occur comparatively infrequently, but efforts are continually being made to devise efficient forecasting techniques. Other hazards have more far-reaching effects. For example, although the floods in Florence in 1966 did not cause many deaths, the cost of damage to private property and art treasures such as books and paintings has been estimated at $1500 million (£625 million). It is virtually impossible to plan defenses against such extremes, but warning systems might be introduced so that people and property could be moved before the same thing happens again. Less dramatic, but no less important in its effects, is a drought, such as the one in Bihar, India, that started in 1965. It affected over half the people in the state and meant that the 1966 rice crop was less than one quarter of the normal annual return. Starvation was widespread and one estimate put the number of deaths caused by the drought conditions at almost 2,000,000.

A further major hazard is the loss due to pests and diseases, both of which are heavily dependent on weather conditions. In mid-latitude countries, weather-sensitive diseases such as potato blight, apple scab, and liver fluke have attracted the attention of research workers. In tropical areas, the movement and distribution of desert locusts are determined to a

very large extent by the patterns of airflow. The last two major hazards are gales and associated effects of snow and frost. Most damage caused by gales is the flattening of crops and trees and the lifting of roofs from buildings. Fortunately gales can be forecast quite accurately and most buildings are designed to withstand them. Snow and frost not only greatly hamper farming operations but can even cause the death of hundreds of animals. In contrast to gales, snow is difficult to forecast, particularly its amount and location, and this makes it virtually impossible to provide a forecast of the potential hazard.

The obvious effects on agriculture of all these hazards, both local and widespread, can be measured in monetary terms. The United States Department of Agriculture says that the annual losses in agriculture in the country averaged more than $13 billion during the years 1942–51 and that 11 per cent of this was caused directly by weather. On a more constructive note, it is estimated that by using weather forecasts farmers in the United Kingdom achieve an increase in productivity of £20 million a year and that if meteorological advice were fully used it could save up to £100 million a year, or 5 per cent of the annual value of agricultural production in the United Kingdom. To overcome the hazards and to increase productivity in any country requires the introduction of a special weather service for agriculture. The aims of such a service are to suggest means of protection against weather hazards, thus reducing costs of production; to provide forecasts in order to increase the efficiency of planting, disease or insect control, and harvesting; and to investigate relationships between physical environment and the quality of the plant or animal product. Obviously, both short-term and long-term forecasts are useful—the first is an important factor to be considered in any decision on planting and harvesting schedules on a day-to-day basis, and the second is of great value in making operational planning possible for months ahead.

Most weather services give an agricultural forecast in terms of the weather to be expected over the next week. This is only one of the predictions made by the United States Weather Bureau Agricultural Weather Service. The shortest term forecast issued by this Service is one of precipitation during the next one to six hours. Such information allows large outdoor machine operations to be delayed and indoor work to be undertaken. For example, if rain is forecast, spraying of crops must be postponed, because the spray would be washed off the trees and plants. The general agricultural weather forecast is a two-day one, giving expected amounts, durations, and intensities of cloud, precipitation, wind, dew, temperatures, and humidities. The third forecast issued by this Service is a five-day outlook; in essence, this is the type of forecast given to farmers in the United Kingdom by the British Meteorological Office. The thirty-day forecast for farmers is the last and least reliable type issued by the Agricultural Weather Service. All these forecasts are concerned with several parameters that affect most agricultural practices. It is of course possible to prepare even more specialized forecasts for individual operations, such as crop dusting and spraying, or the decision to irrigate.

Transport and Industry

Despite the increasing complexity and capabilities of modern transport systems, the direct effects on them of weather cannot be ignored: indeed, they are often forcibly brought to our attention when some extreme of the weather occurs. Certain weather elements affect all types of transport to a similar degree, others are peculiar to one particular type. Perhaps the most frequent and widespread hazard is fog, which often brings all air traffic to a standstill and reduces the efficiency of shipping and road and rail transport. Several densities of fog are recognized and this is a great help in assessing the hazard. In aviation, for instance, even light fogs (defined by WMO as those limiting visibility to 1000 meters) can be critical at high speeds, whereas on roads and railways even a dense fog (40 m. visibility) may not cause a complete standstill, though it may well lead to accidents.

The heavy dependence of air traffic on weather conditions is emphasized by the presence of a meteorological station at most large airports. Such stations not only take observations for the national, central meteorological office, but also make their own forecasts of conditions for the immediate vicinity of the airport. Their main concern is with visibility, cloud ceiling, and local turbulence—all critical factors in the takeoff and landing of aircraft. There are other elements, such as slush on the runway, that may have disastrous effects. Once in the air, aircraft are very much at the mercy of the weather. Wherever possible a flight path will take advantage of tailwinds and avoid headwinds to make the most efficient use of its fuel; but this requires accurate knowledge of wind flow over a very large area. On a more local scale, turbulence within the atmosphere can lead to an uncomfortable ride, and in its most violent forms can have devastating effects. It is most readily seen in cloud form, but it may also occur in the lee of mountain barriers and in the vicinity of the *jet stream* (see diagram on page 89) that blows high in the *troposphere* (the layer of the atmosphere extending from 10 to 20 km. above sea level). Clear air turbulence, for obvious reasons, is often the most dangerous to aircraft. A further hazard to aircraft flying in the troposphere is ice formation on the wings and fuselage. This occurs when supercooled droplets in clouds freeze on the aircraft surface. If the droplets are large, they may spread before freezing, giving rise to clear ice; small droplets tend to freeze immediately in the form of rime ice. Clear ice is by far the most dangerous type, because it forms readily at temperatures between $0°$ and $-10°$c and, being of high density, interferes with the weight and aerodynamic properties of the aircraft.

Weather hazards in industry and transport. Left: high wind completely destroyed this cooling tower at an electrical power station in northern England in 1965. Right: total cost of bad weather to scheduled airlines in the United States during 1965 was estimated at $97 million. This BEA plane landing on a beach in the Hebrides, where there is no alternative landing strip, is completely dependent on weather and tidal conditions. Far right: sudden or flash flooding following torrential rain in Western Australia.

All these examples show the extent of the dependence of aviation on weather, and most national meteorological services spend a substantial proportion of their resources on the provision of forecasts for air traffic. Over half the annual budget of the British Meteorological Office, for example, is spent on services for the RAF and civil aviation.

The interaction between atmosphere and ocean has always been a potential hazard to shipping. Perhaps the most significant meteorological parameter is wind speed. Even large ocean liners experience significant differences between their performances in headwinds and in tailwinds. The state of the sea is now considered to be a function of the wind's speed, constancy, *fetch* (distance over which ocean waves are generated by the wind), and duration, and the temperature difference between air and water. All these are easily observable parameters, and forecasts based on meteorological data are now made of "danger areas" in the oceans. Fog, ice loading, frozen sea surface, and icebergs are also potential shipping hazards.

Whereas aircraft are readily grounded by weather conditions and ships often have to shelter in harbors, rail and road transport are more tolerant of extremes. It has been shown that trains can and do operate in any winds of less than hurricane force (over 65 knots); rainfall and humidity have no marked effect; and in some parts of the world, tracks are kept open through the heaviest snowfalls and through drifts of 6–10 m. in

depth. The worst effects usually occur when the particular weather phenomenon is rather infrequent. There were, for instance, long delays to trains caused by drifting snow in the winter of 1962–3 in Great Britain, but a winter of such severity had not occurred for over 200 years and consequently British Rail were not prepared for it. The minor hazards of track expansion at high temperatures (those above 37.8°c) and increasing rail brittleness at temperatures between −12.2° and −31.7°c are easily overcome by careful design, but even this is often ignored in road construction. *Frost heaving* (lifting of surfaces caused by the expansion of ice in the soil) can cause substantial damage to the road surface, and to avoid this it is important to lay the ballast section of roads in dry, nonfreezing conditions. Fog, high winds, and ice are greater hazards on roads than on railroads, particularly to fast-moving freeway traffic. Ice is a slightly less frequent, but by no means less dangerous, hazard than fog, and occurs in its most widespread form with freezing drizzle or rain. Conditions of this kind can cause an increase in accidents of as much as 70 per cent.

In theory, it is possible to maintain life and the necessities of life at virtually any extreme of weather conditions. Whether it would be economic to do so is a very different matter. Nevertheless, weather is an important consideration in industrial planning, particularly in the design and planning of a new plant. Elements that commonly hold up industrial operations are extreme temperature, snow, sleet, ice, high wind, heavy rainfall, high humidity, and poor visibility. Of these, low temperatures probably have the most widespread effects. Temperatures below freezing create many problems in industries that are unprepared for such extremes. The freezing of water is a common problem, but there are many others—the freezing-up of building sites, difficulty in starting unprotected machines, unworkable materials, and a marked drop in labor efficiency to 50 per cent of normal at 0°C, and 25 per cent at —12°C. Industries that are prepared for cold weather operations and, like some railroads, are experienced in dealing with such conditions, usually suffer only minor inconveniences. There is, however, an absolute limitation imposed by low temperature and it is generally accepted that the lowest temperature at which any economic activity can be continued on a useful basis is about —46°C. The effects of high temperature do not appear to be as marked as those of the opposite extreme. Even in desert locations, work days are more often lost as a result of sandstorms than because of high temperature alone. The decline in efficiency that does occur seems to be a result of human body reactions rather than of equipment.

Within the extremes illustrated so far, changes in temperature can be vitally important, particularly for the industries that supply heat. In the United Kingdom, industries supplying electricity and gas are particularly sensitive to temperature changes. A fall of 1°C in air temperature usually increases the load on the electricity network by 1.3 per cent in summer and 1.8 per cent in winter. More accurate forecasts of temperature would obviously allow the present necessary reserve to be decreased to make a substantial saving.

Sleet or freezing fog can make construction work extremely difficult and all work usually stops until the ice melts. Wind and rainfall are also responsible for delays in building, and rainfall, in the long run, determines the availability of water for industrial processes and domestic use. High relative humidities impose comparatively minor impairments on most industrial activities; it is their influence on the workers that reduces productivity. There are, however, a few industrial processes that are adversely affected by high relative and absolute humidities: for instance, blast furnace efficiency decreases significantly with high absolute humidity. It is generally agreed that the critical figure for impairment to economic activity is 80 per cent relative humidity.

These widespread effects of weather on agriculture, transport, and industry, and upon man himself, explain why forecasting is still the prime task of the world's meteorological centers. The weather forecasts provided by·these organizations may be for periods ranging from one hour to one month ahead, covering distances ranging from a few to thousands of kilometers. They serve military and civil aviation, agriculture, shipping, industry, and commerce, and in some cases provide a personal service. In Britain, the Meteorological Office provides information about prolonged fine spells or severe frosts to individual subscribing farmers. In North America, the United States Department of Commerce issues a Weekly Weather and Crop Bulletin which contains a review of precipitation and temperature conditions for a week, covering all states of the Union. This is only one example of the many types of service, apart from general forecasting, provided by most national meteorological centers. Each year, millions of inquiries about the weather are received by these centers from industry and the public. In 1965 the British Meteorological Office answered 1.16 million inquiries—those from industry including questions about rainfall, runoff, and evaporation from engineers engaged in dam construction; from architects designing high buildings about wind loading; and from the planners of new towns about general climatic factors. The financial return from such specialized forecasts can be impressive: in the United States it has been estimated that the value of accurate, reliable five-day forecasts to agriculture, transport, and water management alone would be as much as $5700 million—that is, 24 times the cost of weather services in the United States during 1966 and over 100 times the United States's contribution to the World Weather Watch. The core of any meteorological service, therefore, is weather forecasting on many scales of time and space. In the following chapters we shall see how this is done.

2 Observation

As individuals, our awareness of weather is dominated by our sensitivity to temperature, rainfall, sunshine, and extremes of wind speed. Although records of rainfall occurrence and wind direction were kept on a daily basis as early as the 14th century, it was only with the invention of the thermometer and barometer in the first half of the 17th century that instrumental measurements could be made. Rainfall was first recorded in England toward the end of the 17th century, but until the middle of the 19th century most observations were made by individuals on their own initiative. The first gathering of weather observations on an international scale was by a Frenchman, the Chevalier de Lamarck, between 1800 and 1815. But it was only with the foundation of national meteorological centers, such as the British Meteorological Office in 1854 and the United States Weather Bureau (as part of the U.S. Army Signal Service) in 1870, that observation of the weather took on both an organized and a widespread form.

Satellite photographs like this one (taken at a height of 350 km.) of a storm center near the Strait of Gibraltar (Spain is on the left, Morocco on the right) have revolutionized weather observation. Two new cloud patterns have been identified: cellular, seen in the foreground of the picture, and banded, as in the swirling storm center.

The essentials of the routines formulated in the second half of the 19th century remain the basis of surface weather observation. But with the invention and increasing use of aircraft in the 20th century, the necessity for observations and forecasts of the state of the troposphere throughout its 10–20 km. depth has been recognized. The organization of upper-air soundings in Europe was given an impetus by aircraft requirements during World War II, and postwar cooperation through the WMO has led to a worldwide network of stations including permanent weather ships, the first of which were established in the Atlantic in 1947. It is this regular sampling of atmospheric characteristics by surface and upper-air stations that provides most of our data for weather analysis and forecasting. This chapter outlines the techniques employed.

Routine Surface Observation

Surface weather observation involves the measurement of certain parameters that, taken together, give a reasonably full description of the meteorological state of the lower atmosphere at any one time. The most familiar parameters are pressure, temperature, humidity, cloudiness, visibility, wind, precipitation, and sunshine; these form the core of the many possible elements that may be observed. The inclusion of visibility as a regular observation is largely to meet aviation requirements but, as we saw in the previous chapter, it is also important for many surface activities. Pressure is the parameter that forms the basis of most synoptic or overall analyses (in meteorology, *synoptic* analysis means the use of meteorological data obtained simultaneously over a wide area for the purpose of presenting a comprehensive and, as near as possible, instantaneous picture of the state of the atmosphere). The other elements, which can be sensed directly, are usually known as the actual "weather."

Surface weather-observing stations may be classified according to the number of atmospheric parameters they observe and the frequency with which they observe them. A fully equipped synoptic station observes an impressive list of parameters every specified observing time, which is sometimes every hour or even half hour throughout the day; other smaller stations observe a selection of the list only once a day. In our consideration of the instruments and techniques employed in the observations, however, we shall take as our model the full synoptic station. The parameters observed at a standard full synoptic station are as follows:

Present weather
Wind direction and speed
Amount of cloud
Total cloud
Amount of low cloud
Amount of low individual cloud layer or mass
Forms of cloud
Height of cloud base
Visibility
Dry bulb temperature
Wet bulb temperature
Barometric tendency and characteristic
Barometric pressure
Past weather
State of ground
Rainfall
Extreme temperature (maximum or minimum)
Grass minimum temperature
Earth temperature
Duration of bright sunshine
Sudden changes in any element between observing times

Some of these observations are made by instruments and some by eye. The instrumental observations are accurate only for the lowest layers of the atmosphere over a restricted area, whereas the estimates, such as that of cloud amount, are relevant to a much larger area than the immediate surroundings of the station. Despite these qualifications, all measurements must be taken as representative of a much larger area than the one they sample directly.

The instrumental observations include the measurement of pressure, temperatures and humidities, wind speed and direction, precipitation, duration of bright sunshine, and perhaps cloud heights and speeds. *Pressure* is measured in millibars and

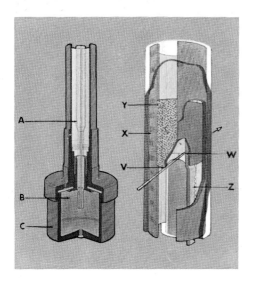

Operation of a mercury-in-glass-tube barometer, seen in section. When the mercury level in the tube (A) falls, the level (B) in the stainless steel cistern (C) rises. Therefore the distance between B and the level in the tube is shorter than it would be if measured directly. The scale intervals are therefore contracted to take account of the relative diameters of cistern and tube. Reading is done by adjusting level of vernier scale (Y) by means of the toothed rack (Z) until edges (V and W) are in line with the top of mercury column. Main scale (X) is then read to nearest millibar and vernier scale to nearest tenth of a millibar.

tenths, corrected for temperature and, because pressure falls with height, observed values are also corrected for station altitude to give the values that would be observed at mean sea level (average surface atmospheric pressure is about 1013 mb.). The tendency of the pressure field—that is, whether pressure has risen or fallen in the past three hours—is also recorded. These measurements are made at all weather-observing stations that record more than once a day, but there are some special observations that are only necessary at airports. These are the pressure at airfield level and readings for aircraft altimeter settings. This last is the value of pressure for a particular airfield and time that, when set on the subscale of an altimeter (based on the international standard atmosphere), will cause the altimeter to read the height of the airfield when the aircraft is at rest on the runway.

The instruments used to record pressure are of two main types: the mercury-in-glass-tube barometer for accurate readings of pressure at any one time; and the barograph, usually of the aneroid type, which records the variation of pressure with time. The readings on the mercury barometer are taken to one-tenth of a millibar, and a thermometer on the barometer, plus a knowledge of the height of the mercury cistern above mean sea level, allows correction to be made for temperature and altitude. A barometer of this type is shown on this page. Barographs are far less accurate in their readings but are very useful for assessing

Aneroid barograph and trace. A series of aneroid vacuum chambers (center), which deflate with increased pressure, is connected to a magnifying linkage. This moves the pen against the chart which slowly rotates, usually making one complete turn every seven days. The trace below records a week in which pressure at the beginning was high with anticyclonic conditions, resulting in fine weather.

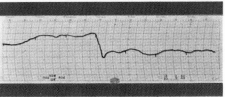

pressure tendencies. Exact compensation for temperature has proved to be very difficult to attain, and it is important to remember, as in all autographic instruments, that frequent time marks should be made on the chart.

Temperature and humidity measurements use the familiar dry and wet bulb thermometers, whereas maximum, minimum, and soil temperatures are taken on especially constructed thermometers. Readings are made to the nearest tenth of a degree, either Fahrenheit (as in the United States) or centigrade (as in most European countries). In this book temperatures throughout are expressed in the more widely used centigrade scale. The dry bulb, and wet bulb, maximum, and minimum thermometers are all housed in a louvered screen, partly to protect them from the other elements, but mainly to ensure that the true (shade) air temperature is measured. Earth temperatures are taken at 30 cm., 60 cm., and 120 cm., with thermometers suspended in iron tubes, whereas those at 10 cm., or 20 cm., below the surface are registered on a bent stem thermometer. The temporal variations of air temperature are noted on a thermograph, the most common type being the bimetallic one. The mechanism depends on the different coefficients of expansion of two strips of metal; this causes a coil of such metals to open or close in response to variations in temperature, and a system of levers translates this curling into a pen trace (see page 33). The autographic trace of relative humidity is recorded on a hygrograph (see page 33), often using a human hair as its sensor. Hair length varies considerably with relative humidity but only very little with other meteorological elements. *Wind speed and direction* are probably the two most fickle atmospheric characteristics. Because of the rapid variation of wind speed with height, all observations are corrected to what the wind speed would be at the standard height of 10 m. The unit of speed is the *knot* (one nautical mile or 1853.2 m. per hour), and direction is given in degrees from true north. Wind direction is determined by the use of a vane and the measurement is made either by simply observing the vane or by a continuous trace on an especially drawn chart. Wind speed is measured by cup anemometers and pressure tube anemometers. The cup anemometer works by the wind causing three hemispherical cups to spin around a vertical axis. The most frequent way of taking a measurement on this type of anemometer is to let the spin of the cups drive a small electric generator; this provides a current, which is indicated or recorded by a meter, the scale of which is calibrated in terms of wind speed. Pressure tube anemometers use a combination of pressure and suction forces to measure wind speed. The orifice is kept toward the wind by a vane, and holes in the supporting vertical tube provide the suction head. The two forces work together to move a float in a cistern, and a pen attached to this float gives a record of the wind speed in knots on a calibrated chart.

Measurement of *precipitation* involves the simplest of all techniques. A container is left out for a given period, usually 24 hours, and the depth of collected water is measured. A typical rain gauge (see page 32) stands 30 cm. above the ground, has an orifice of 13 cm. diameter and a funnel leading to a jar that collects the water; the jar itself stands in a can, which collects any possible surplus. Several variations on this theme are to be found, however. If the gauge is to be sited in a particularly wet or inaccessible area that cannot be visited for periods of up to a month, then its capacity is increased. The amount of rain is established with the use of the rain measure, which may have more than one design and may be graduated in either millimeters or inches.

The variation of rainfall over a period of time is recorded on a chart in a fashion similar to that of temperature, pressure, or humidity. Recording rain gauges give a continuous record of rainfall and also supply two types of information: the total amount of rainfall in unit time between observing hours, and the rate at which rain falls. The basic mechanism of recording rain gauges is to monitor a certain amount of rainfall until the receiving chamber is full, and then quickly get rid of this water by siphoning or simply tipping out so that the process may start again. The trace from a siphoning type of gauge is shown on page 32. The steepness of the trace is an indication of the rate of rainfall, and the total amount should be checked against a nearby ordinary daily gauge. Using the tilting bucket principle, a new type of rain gauge has been designed that allows interrogation by telephone. Each time the bucket tips when it is full, an electric pulse is received by a counting device and, on interrogation by telephone, the number of pulses is given by "pips." As the size of the bucket is known, it is possible to work out how much rain has fallen since the counter was set at zero. This type of gauge is still being perfected but it will have tremendous value in inaccessible areas.

The measurements of *duration of bright sunshine* and *height of cloud base* are of similar simplicity. The first of these is carried out by means of a glass sphere that concentrates the sun's rays onto a card on which a scorched trace (due to the sun's apparent movement) is produced for as long as bright sunshine lasts. The standard recorders make allowance for latitude and season, so that measurement is simply a matter of establishing the length of the burn. Cloud base height may be measured by timing a constant lift balloon or, at night, by the use of a vertical searchlight and scanner. If neither of these methods is possible, cloud base must be estimated. The assessment of the total amount of cloud consists in estimating how much of the total apparent area of the sky, to the nearest eighth, is covered with cloud. Cloud observation is completed by the recognition of the forms of cloud present, the determination of the direction from which the clouds are moving, and a measurement or estimate of their speed of motion.

Above left: a standard thermometer screen. The two vertical thermometers are dry bulb (left), giving ordinary air temperature, and wet bulb (right) which has its bulb covered with wet muslin. Difference in temperature between the two provides data from which relative humidity is calculated. Other instruments are thermograph (which continuously records temperature) and hygrograph (which registers humidity changes). Above right: cup contact anemometer measures wind speed. As cups revolve, a switch is closed at fixed intervals: speed can be measured by counting the intervals.

Below left: the natural siphon rainfall recorder, shown here with lid off, records time, rate, duration, and total of rainfall. Below right: operation of the recorder. Rain falls through rim (A) and is caught in funnel below: it then enters chamber (B) through filter (C). This makes float (D) rise so that pen (E) writes on chart wrapped around rotating drum. Water then rises in float chamber (B) and up side tube (F) until float reaches point (G) which at once empties chamber so that recording can continue.

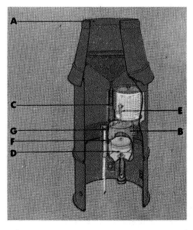

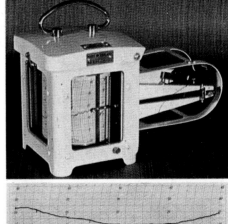

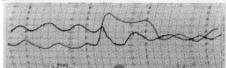

Above: standard sunshine recorder. Glass sphere concentrates sun's rays onto card on which scorched trace (due to sun's apparent movement) is produced while sun is out. Right, top: thermograph records temperature changes between observing hours. This is done by using a bimetallic strip in form of helix. Different coefficients of expansion of the metals cause coil to open or close, thus moving pen over chart on rotating drum. Chart shows dip in temperature after warm spell. Right, center: bimetallic actenograph records variation in intensity of sun's radiation. A bimetallic strip coated with non-reflective black (top of instrument) responds to warmth and records in usual way; two further strips, shaded by white disk, are arranged to bend in opposite directions, thus compensating for variations in air temperature. Right, bottom: thermohygrograph records temperature variations by means of bimetallic strip, but uses bundle of especially treated human hair that changes length with variations in relative humidity. Weekly chart below shows midweek rise in relative humidity (red trace) prior to thunderstorms; cooler weather followed at end of week.

Observations of *visibility* and *state of the ground* depend on visual impression. Visibility is usually assessed by the observation of objects at known distances from the station, but visibility meters are particularly useful at night. These use photoelectric cells and are of two types: those that measure the attenuation coefficient of a long column of air, and those that measure the scattering of light from a small volume of air. State of the ground is given on a scale of zero to nine, ranging from "surface of ground dry" to "loose dry snow, dust, or sand covering ground completely." As this scale was devised for mass observation it is necessarily simple and, to a certain extent, allows the subjectivity of the observer to influence the quality of the observation.

The remaining noninstrumental surface observations are included in the record of "present" and "past" weather. This includes such phenomena as precipitation (of all kinds and different degrees of intensity), thunder, lightning, squalls, mist, fog, frosts, and a comment on the state of the sky. All this information can be expressed in numerical form with the use of the international symbols shown opposite.

The above is a brief review of the measurements and observations taken at full synoptic stations, every half hour at some, but more commonly every three hours from midnight Greenwich Mean Time, the accepted universal time. There is little doubt that the variations in time of one atmospheric element at one place are well recorded, but these are of little use to our understanding of weather unless we have many such stations, all observing with the same regularity, to give us a view over a wide area. This is achieved with a global network of over 7000 land stations and over 4000 merchant and passenger ships that make observations at sea (see map on page 36). The land network is extremely uneven in its coverage. Japan, for example, has one station per 875 km², whereas the Congo has only one station per 45,000 km². The 4000 ships making observations are largely merchant and passenger ships, but there are also weather ships, whose specific task is to provide meteorological observations at the surface and in the upper air at fixed positions in the sea. In the North Atlantic there are nine such ships, four of which are

WW	0	1	2	3	4	5	6	7	8	9
00	◯	◯	◯	◯	⩕	∞	S	$	⧢	(⑀)
10	=	☰	☷	⟨	☺	)•(	( )	⦚	∇	)(
20	⁹]	•]	*]	⁂]	∿]	∇̇]	∇̊]	∇̂]	≡]	⦚]
30	⑀|	⑀	|⑀	⑀|	⑀	|⑀	✛	⧓	†	⧺
40	(≡)	☰	≡|	≡]	☷	≡	|☰	|≡	⊻	⊻
50	⁹	⁹⁹	⁹	⁹⁹	⁹	⁹⁹	∿	∿	⁹	⁹
60	•	••	•	••	•	••	∿	∿	•	⁂
70	✳	✳ ✳	✳	✳ ✳	✳	✳✳	⟷	⟶	⟶	△
80	∇̇	∇̇	∇̇	∇̇	∇̇	∇	∇	∇̂	∇̂	▲
90	∇̂	⦚]	•⦚:	⦚]⧄	⦚]⧄	⦚	⦚	⦚	⦚	⦚

This conversion table lists the internationally accepted symbols for present weather. For transmission by teleprinter, appropriate symbols are converted into figures in black at left and top (thus "snow" becomes 700, 701, 702, and so on, according to density). The figures are then decoded and the symbols plotted at the central meteorological office. A selection of symbols and their meanings is given at right.

⁹ Drizzle (number and position of these in diagram represent different *intensities* and durations)

• Rain („   )

✳ Snow („   )

▲ Hail

⁂ Sleet

∇ Shower (Thus ∇̇ rep. rain shower)

☰ Fog (Variations represent differences in intensity)

⟨ Lightning

⦚ Thunderstorm

∿ Glazed frost

⑀ Duststorm or Sandstorm

The surface network of 7000 observing stations provides most of the raw data for weather analysis and forecasting. The map shows most of the stations at which normal synoptic surface observations should be made every three hours and internationally exchanged under WMO agreements. In fact, just over 90 per cent of the stations shown fulfill WMO requirements.

2000 km

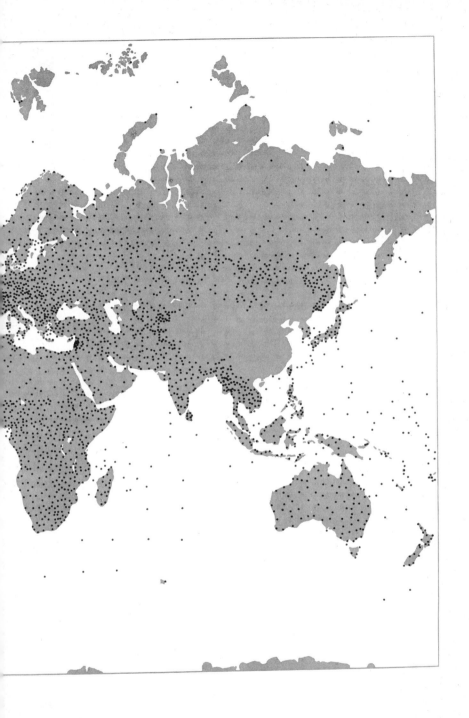

maintained by the United States and the remainder jointly looked after by Britain, France, the Netherlands, Norway, and Sweden. To keep a station running requires more than one ship and in fact Britain now has four, based at Greenock in Scotland. All these ships observe cloud height and type, wind speed and direction, pressure, visibility, temperature, humidity, sea temperature, and the direction, height, and periodicity of waves every hour, as well as sending up balloons every 6 hours for observation of the upper winds, and radiosondes every 12 hours.

Routine Upper Air Observation

Most surface observations are taken to describe the atmospheric characteristics in the immediate surrounds of the station, so that much of the atmosphere is, in fact, observed indirectly. Thus many weather phenomena may be incompletely described or totally ignored—a situation that can be partly remedied by the use of radar and electronic storm-detecting (sferic) equipment. Both observation methods are capable of instantaneous, objective, large-area coverage and, as such, are powerful tools in weather analysis and forecasting. Radar is widely used for routine forecasting, as well as for research into cloud physics and dynamics. Since 1945 many radar systems have been especially designed to detect clouds of precipitation particles. Since that time, radar has been used to such an extent that a whole field of radar meteorology has developed. It has been primarily concerned with the many problems of severe storms, but radar is used daily in routine forecasting in many countries, including the United States and the United Kingdom.

Reflected energy provides the basis of all radar. The amount of energy reflected from a raindrop depends on a number of factors, but to a large extent the size, or more particularly the diameter, of a drop governs the amount of back-scattered energy. In fact, for a given wavelength, the back-scattered energy is proportional to the sixth power of the drop diameter. So for a constant drop diameter a shorter wavelength results in a higher reflection. A third important influence on the amount of received energy is that of attenuation—that is, the weakening of the outgoing and reflected wave by intervening clouds and raindrops. The shorter the wavelength, the greater the attenuation. This may lead to a conflict of opinion as to which is the more useful radar: a shortwave device to detect very small drops but subject to strong attenuation, or a comparatively longwave set to cover large raindrop sizes with little attenuation. In fact, several wavelengths are used.

The range of radar wavelengths extends from 23 cm. to 0.8 cm. and they all have an optimum target. The 23-cm. set is used primarily for detection of aircraft and is not designed for weather detection, being useful only for finding the general location of precipitation areas. The 10-cm. wavelength is much more suited to the detection of precipitation, and together with the 3-cm. wavelengths is used most frequently in routine operations. The 1.25-cm. and 0.8-cm. wavelengths are used mainly for research into cloud physics and dynamics.

Whatever the wavelength of the radar, the information is displayed on a cathode-ray tube. The displays are of three major types: the *plan position indicator* (PPI); the *range height indicator* (RHI); and the *signal amplitude-range indicator* (A-scope). The plan position indicator is the most common form of presentation used for weather radar information. It is, in fact, virtually a map of echoes at any one time (see display illustrated on page 40). This is supplemented by the range height indicator, which gives a section of precipitating clouds along a chosen line (see also page 40). Usually the aerial sweeps through angles of elevation from about $-2°$ to about $+45°$ to the horizontal. As is evident from the picture on page 40, the vertical height scale is considerably magnified compared with the range scale. The range of both displays depends on the particular instrument in use, but it is usually 200–300 km. on the PPI and somewhat less on the RHI; the vertical range of the RHI covers the 15 km. or so of troposphere. The last of these systems, the signal amplitude-range indicator, is used infrequently and gives a measure of the range of an object along a central horizontal line, as well as the intensity of the echo by its length in the vertical (see page 40).

The best way to record radar information permanently is by

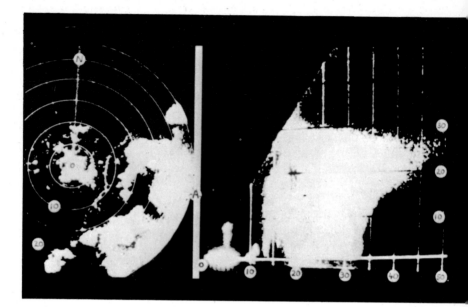

Above: a heavy rainstorm is shown in plan view on the screen of a plan position indicator radar (PPI) and in side elevation on a range height indicator (RHI). Whiteness of areas depends upon varying intensity of echoes from precipitation: figures at base of both scopes give range from radar station in miles, those at right on RHI height in thousands of feet. Below left: diagrammatic representation of signal amplitude range indicator (A-scope) screen. This gives measure of range of object along horizontal line, and intensity of echo by its vertical height. Below right: diagram shows typical PPI display that has been digitized according to intensity of echoes to facilitate communication.

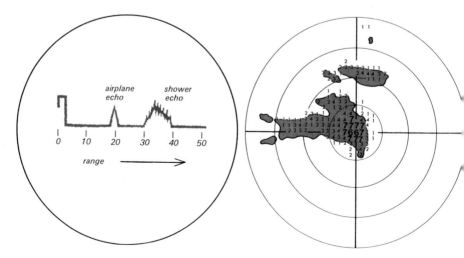

taking a photograph of the scope. Such a record is invaluable to the research worker but is of little use to the forecaster. To quote a recent report: "The use of radars in both scales (local area and large) involves the difficulties of translating a series of visual presentations showing shape, size, three-dimensional extent, movement intensity, and changes of all these into meaningful symbols or displays for transmission to remote locations." The codes used to do this vary from country to country, and attempts have recently been made to reduce the subjectivity that creeps into any description of an echo distribution. Devices that automatically digitize displays are available (see opposite) but they suffer from a loss of detail in echo patterns resulting from the relatively coarse grids that must be used in encoding.

By far the greatest number of operational and research weather radar systems are to be found in the United States and northwest Europe (see map on page 45). In the United States a network of about 100 sets is operated by the Environmental Science Services Administration (ESSA). These sets are used for both routine forecasting and research purposes. The radar favored by ESSA is called the WSR-57, a 10-cm. set designed by the United States Weather Bureau. This particular wavelength was chosen because the major function of the radar is the detection of severe storms rather than smaller clouds and light rain; in this way it contrasts with the 3-cm. radars maintained by the British Meteorological Office, for these sets are used to detect showers of a magnitude far less than the severe storms likely to be experienced in North America.

Sferic fixes depend on the radiation of electromagnetic waves caused by lightning flashes in the clouds. The exact location of the lightning flash is fixed by simultaneous observation at a number of different places. In the United Kingdom, for example, where the network was initiated early in World War II, there are four stations; in Cornwall, Northern Ireland, Scotland, and Norfolk. Coverage of Europe is achieved by stations in Gibraltar, Malta, and Cyprus. An example of a sferic plot is illustrated on page 42.

The *radiosonde* is also used to sample upper atmospheric characteristics but it differs from the radar and sferic instru-

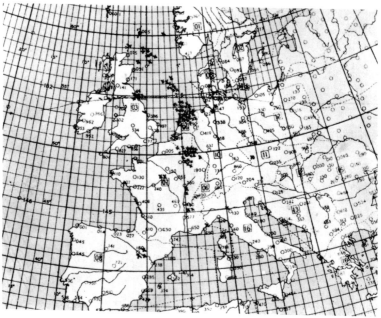

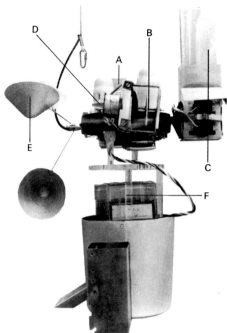

Opposite: plotting a sferic fix. Widely spaced stations pick up electromagnetic waves caused by lightning flashes. By combining directional fixes obtained from a number of stations, it is possible to pinpoint thunderstorms with considerable accuracy. Below: a thunderstorm chart built up by means of sferic plots.

Above left: typical radiosonde balloon with parachute and equipment suspended (distances have been reduced). Right: exploded diagram of actual radiosonde, showing humidity recorder (A), barometric pressure recorder (B), temperature element (C), transmitter (D), windmill to power transmitter (E), and battery (F).

ments in that the information is available in digital rather than visual form. The radiosonde is a balloon to which are attached instruments recording the familiar parameters of pressure, temperature, relative humidity and, indirectly, wind speed and direction at different levels of the atmosphere. In order to do this, the instruments or *sensors* are carried up through the atmosphere until, when the balloon bursts, the sonde falls to earth suspended from a parachute. Although there is a record of one sonde reaching a height of 31,000 m. the more usual altitude is about 18,000 m.

Basically, the sonde converts a meteorological measurement into a musical note, which is then broadcast. The sensors of one

British Meteorological Office sonde, for example, comprise an aneroid capsule for measurement of pressure, a bimetallic coil for temperature, and a strip of gold-beater's skin (the especially prepared outer membrane of the large intestine of an ox) which is sensitive to relative humidity. The values recorded by these sensors activate variable inductors, which produce a signal of varying modulation frequency. The inductors are connected into the circuit about every 6–7 seconds, and pressure, temperature, and humidity readings are taken at height intervals of about 120 m. The observation is made by measuring the modulation frequency of each parameter and converting this into more familiar units of pressure, temperature, and relative humidity. This is achieved at the receiving station, which has three basic instruments: a radio receiver, a cathode-ray oscillograph, and an audio-frequency oscillator. The pattern from the audio-frequency oscillator is varied until it corresponds exactly with the frequency of the signal from the radiosonde, and the frequency is read on the oscillator dial. This observation is plotted against time, started when the sonde left the ground, and the resultant line is referred to a calibration curve to establish the conventional units. The calibration curves are constructed from the results of elaborate tests that subject the sensors, while connected to their sondes, to varying known pressures, temperatures, and humidities. This procedure allows the resultant oscillation frequencies to be measured.

Although great care is taken in these observations, errors—due to the design of the sonde itself—do occur. In an attempt to reduce these errors new types of radiosonde are being tested. In one pre-production model currently being tested, a fine resistance wire is used to sense temperature and an improved aneroid is used to measure pressure; humidity values are still recorded by gold-beater's skin, as in previous designs. In addition, the transmission system has been designed to facilitate automatic handling of data. These new radiosondes however are not yet in routine use.

Slight differences in the actual mechanics of the radiosonde do occur from country to country: for instance, either lithium chloride or a hair may be used as the humidity sensor in one

Opposite: map shows world meteorological rocket network (blue circles represent those making regular soundings, blue squares represent those making intermittent soundings) and world network of principal radar stations (red circles). See page 172 for improvements in this network planned during the World Weather Watch.

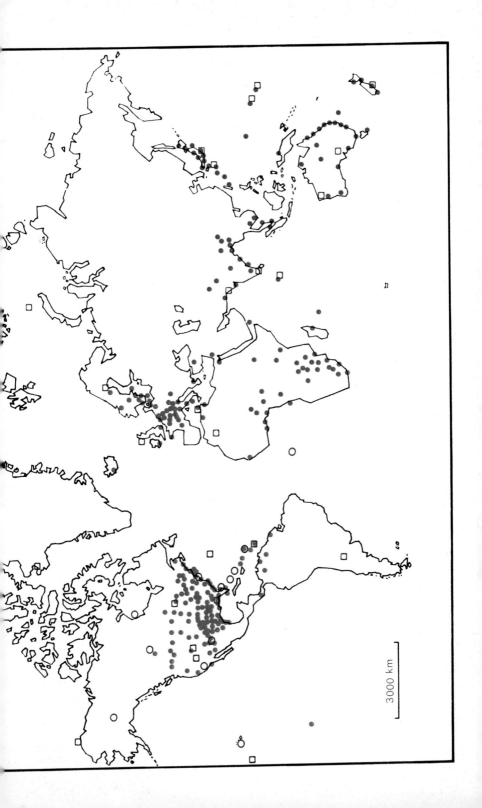

3000 km

United States sonde. Usually, however, the overall procedure is the same the world over, and this extends to the measurement of wind speed and direction by tracking the radiosonde balloon by radar or smaller balloons with a theodolite. The values of temperature, wind speed, wind direction, and height above sea level at a number of standard isobaric surfaces are recorded twice daily at each of the 500 stations in the international network (see map opposite). It is apparent from the frequency of ascents and the density of the upper-air network that our observations of upper-air characteristics are far fewer than those on the surface. Because the three-dimensional description of the atmosphere is dependent on this ascent information, it is not surprising that there is a growing demand for more upper-air stations throughout the world. Some attempts to rectify this situation are outlined in Chapter 6.

Although the greater part of the atmosphere lies below the *tropopause* (the region at the top of the troposphere), which is usually at a pressure of about 200 mb., it is thought that circulations in the *stratosphere* (that is, more than 10–20 km. above the earth's surface) and even the lower *mesosphere* (the layer of atmosphere located more than 400 km. above the earth's surface) may have some influence upon tropospheric systems. We saw that the radiosondes usually reach only the tropopause or slightly higher levels, and are thus incapable of regularly sampling stratospheric levels. Rockets are therefore necessary for taking measurements at altitudes above the tropopause; it is only since 1959, however, that rocket soundings have been coordinated over a large area. This has been made possible by the organization of firing schedules and the general use of standard equipment and methods of data collection. The development of a comparatively inexpensive meteorological rocket that can carry several kilograms to heights of 65 or 70 km., together with new and improved sensors, has allowed contour analyses to be made at the 0.4-mb. level over parts of the rocket network shown on page 45. Two parameters, temperature and wind, are measured at different heights by the use of a sonde that is ejected from the rocket at its apogee. The sampled layer usually extends from about 15 to 65 km. In

Opposite: map shows the impressive world network of principal radiosonde stations. In addition, there are two Arctic and 18 Antarctic stations not shown here.

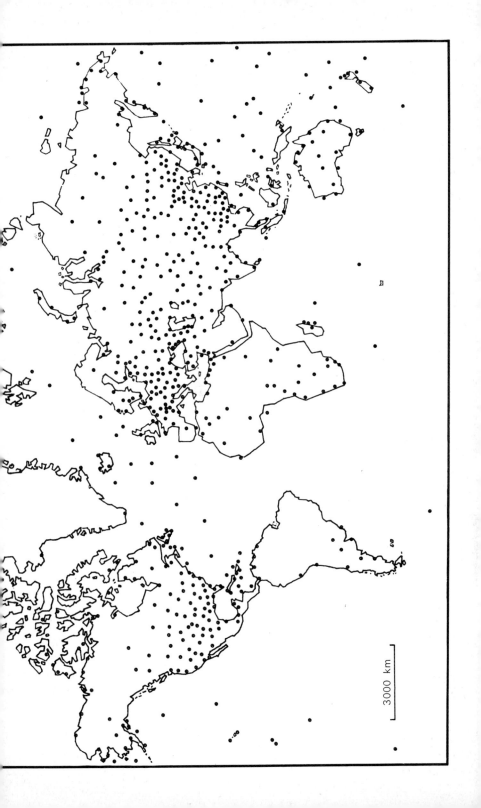

3000 km

the United Kingdom the first results from the SKUA meteorological rocket firings in the Outer Hebrides were recorded in December 1963 from an altitude of 40 km. After a second series of experimental firings in the period from January to April 1965, it was considered that a successful sounding rocket had been developed. An example of the type of temperature profiles recorded by SKUA rockets is shown on this page. The SKUA firings, like most rocket firings for meteorological purposes, are experimental, but it is hoped that the world network shown on page 45 will soon increase in density and that every application of radiosonde data will also be made with rocket sonde information.

Rockets are invaluable for recording and reporting temperature and wind at heights between about 15 and 65 km. Right: the recently developed British SKUA rocket. Components indicated are timing device (A), sonde aerial (B), temperature sensor (C), sonde (D), radar-reflective parachute (E), and motor (F). Below: typical temperature profiles recorded during SKUA trials over the Outer Hebrides during January 1965.

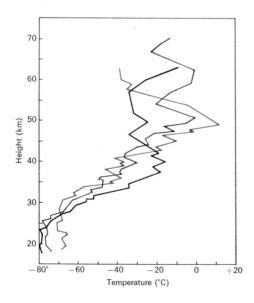

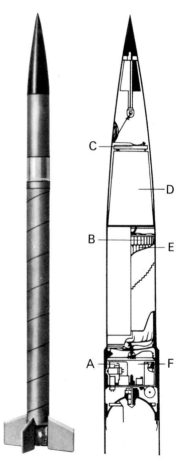

Perhaps the most dramatic breakthrough in the observation of weather phenomena has been the development of the meteorological satellite. It is not necessary to stress how incomplete is our observation, and thus description, of the atmosphere; satellites, by giving us objective, large-area coverage of weather systems, go a long way toward filling the many gaps. Clouds were first photographed from really high altitudes in the 1940s, from rockets fired at the White Sands Range in New Mexico. The significance of these photographs for the meteorologist was first put into print in 1949 with the suggestion that television cameras should be put into the rockets so that the cloud data would be available immediately. It was not until 1954 that the possibilities of a long-duration orbiting satellite were suggested by Dr. H. Wexler of the United States Weather Bureau, but by the time the first Russian Sputnik had been launched in October 1957, plans for meteorological satellites were quite well advanced. Most meteorological satellites have been built and used by scientists working in the United States, and in the absence of any Russian material the following text is based on the American satellite program.

Satellites are capable of obtaining two main types of information: photographs of weather systems made up of various cloud forms, and measurements of radiation, primarily in the infrared. Most of the latter type of information is used in research into the heat balance of the general circulation, whereas most meteorologists hope that cloud photographs, although themselves useful in general meteorological research, will become a routine tool for analysis and forecasting. Although we now receive regular pictures of cloud cover on a world basis, it is only about seven years since the first experiments in this technique were undertaken.

Most of the necessary experimentation was achieved in the series of TIROS (Television and Infrared Observation Satellite) orbits. These satellites weighed about 140 kg. and carried the following equipment: solar cells and storage batteries for power; a stabilization system to determine the direction in which the sensors are looking; command devices and clocks to control the functions of the equipment and its timing; beacon transmitters for tracking the satellite's position; two cameras; radiometers; and radio transmitters and antennas to relay the information to the ground. Once in space they were stabilized in a spin about an axis, which pointed in a fixed direction. This type of stabilization—known as *spin stabilization* (see diagram on page 55)—together with orbit angles of 48° in the first four satellites, meant that coverage of the earth was limited to latitudes equatorward of about 65°, with the cameras pointing toward the earth for only a quarter to a third of each orbit. To acquire the data from TIROS satellites required special Command Data Acquisition (CDA) stations. In the project six stations in the United States were used: at Belmar, New Jersey; Hightstown, New Jersey; Kaena Point, Hawaii; Point Mugu, California; Wallops Island, Virginia; and Fairbanks, Alaska. The received cloud information was used to prepare *nephanalyses* (analyses of cloud systems), and a copy of the first one produced operationally is on page 54. The time involved in storage by the satellite until interrogated and in compiling a nephanalysis often meant that the information was of little use for forecasting. This, however, was overcome in 1963 by the development of automatic picture transmission (APT) in the orbit of *TIROS VIII*. This system enables simple and cheap tracking stations (such as the one illustrated on page 55) to receive pictures directly from the satellites, and, because many of these are being installed around the globe, satellite pictures are becoming available to many forecasters in time to be used in the actual preparation of short-term forecasts.

As a result of the *TIROS I-VIII* orbits, it was possible to launch *Nimbus I* in August 1964 with two important improvements: the satellite was in a near-polar orbit and could therefore observe the entire earth; and it was earth-stabilized so that the cameras and other sensors could always point toward the earth. It took the first extensive worldwide APT pictures. In February 1965 the first complete global coverage of cloud pictures was achieved with *TIROS IX* and the stage was set for the TIROS Operational Satellite (TOS) project to get under way. This began in February 1966 with the launching of *ESSA I* into a near-polar, sun-synchronous circular orbit at a height of 1400 km. and gave the first operationally complete coverage of the globe on a daily basis. A second satellite, *ESSA II*, was launched in February 1966, and this was again in a near-polar orbit. It was the first operational satellite to incorporate APT, and up to nine pictures could be received by the simple ground stations with a directional aerial, receiver, and facsimile recorder. *ESSA II* orbited at a height of about 1400 km. with a period of 113 minutes and took pictures every 352 seconds. *ESSAs I* and *II* were replaced by *ESSAs III* and *IV*, launched in October 1966 and January 1967 respectively and these too were replaced by *ESSAs V* and *VI* later in 1967. *Nimbus II*, launched in May 1966, carries an experimental night-time readout system, known as DRIR (direct readout infrared), as well as the day time APT system.

Up to December 1965, meteorological satellites provided over half a million television pictures and over 5000 transmissions of infrared data for research. These observation platforms in space are helping to fill vast gaps in the conventional earthbound weather observation network. The next job is to devise techniques for obtaining routine information from satellites in terms of conventional meteorological parameters and for applying this information in daily operations. Some ways in which satellite photographs have already significantly aided analysis and forecasting are given in Chapters 3 and 4.

Nonroutine Observation

Weather observation has come a long way since its humble 19th-century beginnings, but the routine methods described so far do not quite complete the picture. The rocket network, as we have already seen, is one method of observation that is also used in nonroutine atmospheric research; there are a number of others that are used primarily for this purpose. Three typical methods are special networks of surface stations, aircraft fitted with instruments, and cloud photogrammetry.

Most observation techniques for research purposes are developed to solve a specific problem: there are consequently nearly as many techniques as there are research projects. The simplest refinement of routine observations for research pur-

Left: launching of NASA's TIROS I, the first meteorological satellite, into orbit in April 1960 opened up a new dimension in world weather observation. Opposite: photographs taken from TIROS satellites in 1961 and 1962 show changes in cloud distribution associated with development of the familiar depression. They confirm accuracy of traditional methods of analysis described in Chapter 3. Picture A shows an open wave form, corresponding to the cold front (blue) and warm front (red). Picture B shows beginning of occlusion process (cold front catching up with warm front). Pictures C and D show further development and maximum intensity of occlusion, and pictures E and F the weakening occlusion and final dissipation of the depression.

poses is the increase in the density of surface station networks involved in mesometeorological and micrometeorological studies. (*Mesometeorology* is that branch of the science concerned with the study of atmospheric phenomena and weather systems with diameters of about 150 km.; *micrometeorology* is concerned with smaller scale phenomena and systems, usually within the surface boundary layer.) This increased density depends entirely upon the scale of the disturbances to be studied. As a result of his investigations, Dr. T. Fujita of the University of Chicago has identified three densities of mesometeorological network. They are the coarse network with an average station spacing of about 50 km.; the medium network

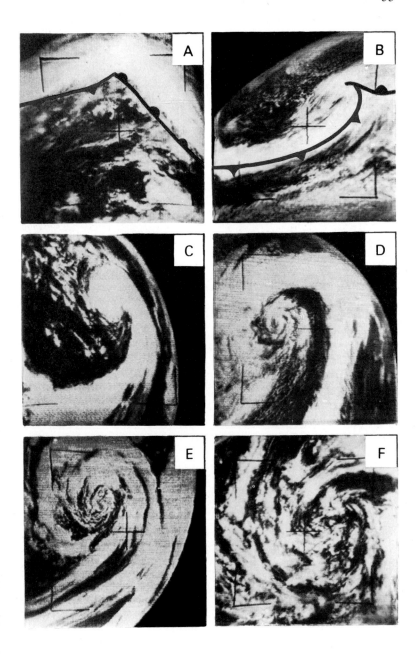

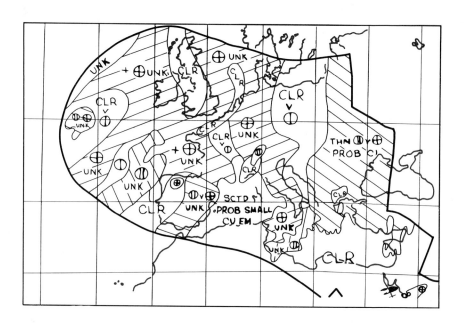

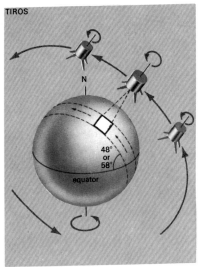

TIROS

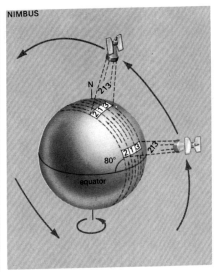

NIMBUS

48°
or
58°

equator

N

213

213

80°

equator

N

Opposite, top: this first operational cloud analysis of a TIROS photograph represents an early attempt to codify such information into a useful, communicable form. Above left: the early spinning, space-orientated TIROS satellites had cameras pointing out through the base plate and could take undistorted vertical observations only once each orbit. Above right: more advanced Nimbus satellite (first launched in 1964) is earth-orientated, has three cameras in fan-like array, and takes continuous photographs of three adjacent strips of earth's surface, from pole to pole, on each orbit. Opposite, below: the geosynchronous ATS I satellite, launched December 1966, provides almost hemispheric photographs such as this one, which shows the Pacific with a storm off the coast of Chile in the lower right area. Right: simple APT ground stations like this one, consisting of a directional aerial, receiver, and facsimile recorder, receive photographs automatically from weather satellites.

Opposite: automatic photographic analysis. Ordinary photographs received from weather satellites can be scanned electronically and the various shades of gray converted into letters and symbols as shown here. A computer can then use these letters and symbols in the numerical forecasting processes described in Chapter 4. Right: most common method of nonroutine observation is simply intensification of surface station network. Map shows network used by the National Severe Storms Project in the southern United States: existing stations shown in red, nonroutine stations in blue.

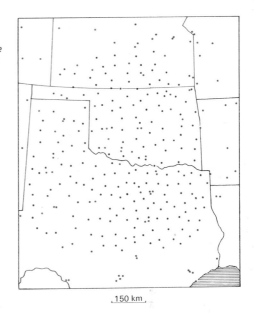

150 km

with spacing of 8 km.; and the fine network with spacing of 1.5 km. A coarse network that was used by the National Severe Storms Project in the United States is illustrated on this page. In fact, most mesometeorological networks are to be found in North America and their objectives are usually convective weather systems. The observed parameters are those covered by ordinary synoptic networks, but usually the instruments are all of the recording type. Thus in the University of Chicago Mesometeorological Project, based at Flagstaff, Arizona, the following instruments were installed in an area 50 × 65 km.: 33 microbarographs; 10 hygrothermographs (instruments for recording humidity and temperature on the same chart); 10 wind recorders; 165 rain gauges; and 165 hail gauges.

Nonroutine coverage of the upper air is much more scanty than that of the surface. One of the most successful ways of filling gaps is to use an aircraft fitted with special instruments. This was recognized in the United Kingdom as early as 1913. It was only after World War II, however, that research into free atmospheric characteristics with the use of instrumented aircraft really got under way. This is well exemplified by the British Meteorological Research Flight (MRF), formed in 1946. The types of observation made by the aircraft may be summarized as follows: measurement of water content of the troposphere and lower stratosphere under various conditions; observation and investigation of temperature, humidity, and wind in the stratosphere in high and low latitudes; exploration of rain-producing clouds; and the investigation of size distribution of water particles in clouds.

A third example of nonroutine observation is cloud photogrammetry. As a result of flights by such units as the MRF, as well as by experimental work in the laboratory and by purely theoretical studies, the mechanics of rain formation are now fairly well understood. Research into the closely allied field of cloud dynamics has for long relied on radar as its main source of evidence, and it is only in the last few years that the potentialities of photography have been realized. Most of this work has been restricted to cumuliform clouds and much of it has been done in the United States. An example of this was the study of cumulus cloud initiation over the Santa Catalina Mountains of Arizona. Two cameras were situated at the ends of a base line about 4 km. long, and directed in parallel lines perpendicular to the base line (see diagram opposite). The field of view of the cameras ensured that the overlap of photographs taken simultaneously by each camera was sufficient for stereoscopic viewing. Stereo pairs, taken at one-minute and two-minute intervals, were analyzed with stereoscope, parallax bar, and ruler, and cloud positions were plotted to accuracies of about 500 m. at a range of 15–30 km. and cloud heights were measured to within 30–60 m. This investigation gave some of the first observations of the direct effects of mountainous terrain upon cloud initiation.

Each of these three nonroutine techniques is an attempt to increase our general understanding of the atmosphere; but none of them can provide the routine, bread-and-butter information that is so vital to weather forecasting. The word "routine" conjures up a picture of repetitive drudgery; and, indeed, some of

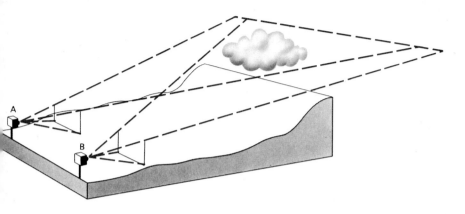

Cloud photogrammetry is a useful nonroutine method of observation. Two identical cameras, A and B, a known distance apart and at the same height, take simultaneous photographs of the same cloud. Using photogrammetrical techniques on the two prints, it is possible to obtain three-dimensional information about the development and growth of the cloud formations.

the schedules may seem to be unduly repetitive to the observer. But the smooth running of a global observational network across all international frontiers is in fact something of which meteorologists may be justly proud. The actual organization of times of observation, elements to be observed, the units and codes to be used, the telecommunications, and similar information is set out in the WMO Technical Regulations. As these Regulations are used by every one of the 132 (in 1967) member countries of WMO, an international standardization has been achieved, and a meteorologist from any country can be sure he will understand all the procedures of any other country. Despite gaps in the global network, it is now possible to describe in reasonable detail the weather patterns over areas of continental dimensions.

3 Analysis

Weather analysis is often thought of as either diagnostic or prognostic, though the distinction is not always clear-cut. The diagnostic approach covers research into the behavior of the atmosphere, often by using analysis of past weather conditions. In prognosis, the description of the present weather situation is used as a basis for forecasting future developments, and it is obviously desirable that this description should be as complete as possible. In Chapter 2 we saw how these facts and figures are accumulated; this chapter deals with their analysis as a prelude to forecasting.

Before looking in detail at the methods used today, let us glance briefly at a few important breakthroughs in weather analysis over the past few decades; in this way we shall see how the fruits of research in one decade become tools of routine analysis in another, and at the same time we shall give historical perspective to our subject. One of the most notable periods in the history of meteorology was the early 1920s, when thought

One of the first steps in all weather analysis is to draw isopleths (lines connecting points of same value) of pressure. The increasing use of automated methods of analysis is aimed at eliminating the subjectivity involved in doing this by hand.

was dominated by a Norwegian research team at Bergen led by Professor V. Bjerknes. These workers introduced into meteorology two important concepts—the air mass and the front.

The *air mass* concept means that an airstream crossing an area at a particular time can be identified by its source region—the area where, through long residence, the temperature and humidity characteristics of the air mass are determined by the nature of the underlying surface. Because certain air masses appeared to be closely related to certain types of weather, the recognition of an air mass and the physical modification that it had undergone on its way from its source region played an important role in the forecasting of the 1930s. They are still used today.

The other important concept introduced by the Norwegians was that of the *front*—a fairly narrow zone of sharp temperature and humidity gradients, often found to be accompanied by extensive cloud and rain. The Bjerknes school suggested that fronts and their weather were due to a simple up-sliding of warmer air masses over a wedge formed by a colder one. It is now realized that the mechanics of fronts are not so simple, but a really satisfactory description of a front in terms of the dynamics of the air motions is still not available. Despite this lack of understanding of frontal dynamics, the empirical relationships between frontal structure and weather sequences established in the 1920s and 1930s are still used by present-day forecasters. For instance, the forecaster knows that an approaching warm front (warm air replacing cold) will probably be preceded by high-level clouds and falling barometer followed by rain and lowering cloud.

Another major breakthrough was the application of *dynamical principles* to the general problem of the development of separate atmospheric systems such as depressions and anticyclones. Much of the early work was done by the British meteorologist R. C. Sutcliffe and today weather analysis and forecasting make extensive use of the basic ideas outlined by Sutcliffe and his collaborators immediately before and after World War II. These workers showed that it was possible to consider the atmosphere as a fluid and, as such, to analyze its

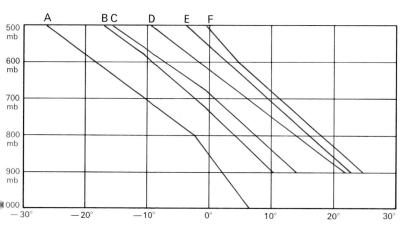

The fact that air masses from different source regions have different characteristics has played an important part in forecasting since the 1930s. Graph shows the range of temperature that can be found in various air masses in summer. Arctic air has 900-mb. temperature of about 4°C and 500-mb. temperature (about 5500 m.) of about −27°C. In contrast, tropical maritime air has temperatures of 25°C and 0°C at the same levels.

A Arctic Air
  Murmansk and Archangel

B Polar Maritime Air
  West Germany and France

C Polar Continental Air
  Helsinki, Utti, and Slutsk

D Tropical Continental Air
  Moscow, Smolensk, and Cracow

E Monsoon Air
  Madras

F Tropical Maritime Air
  Pensacola

motions with the use of the classical equations of fluid dynamics. In itself this was nothing new, but in its application to forecasting it was quite revolutionary. Here at last the forecaster had the beginnings of a theoretical approach to weather systems that could be used in actual forecasting. As we review various analytical techniques, the importance of the work of the Norwegians and of Sutcliffe will soon become apparent.

Communications

Before any analysis of the weather can be made, the observations from the surface and upper-air networks must be assembled in a suitable form for the analyst, who is usually a forecaster.

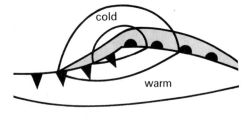

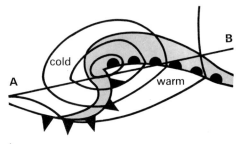

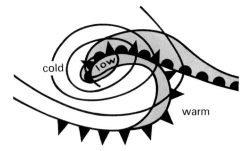

Fronts and frontal depressions have been the real foundation of mid-latitude forecasting since the early 1920s. Left: plan-view development of a frontal depression as depicted by Bjerknes in 1922. Warm front is shown by rounded symbols, cold by spiked symbols, and cloud area in blue. The lines are isobars. Relatively warm and cold air is indicated. (See the satellite photographs on page 53 for comparison.) Below: cross section of a typical frontal depression (equivalent to AB on plan view above) based on recent information from research flights. C indicates a zone of transition from moist to dry air above the cold frontal zone, causing clouds to occur ahead of the zone itself. D shows the position of the jet stream (a river of rapidly moving air as diagramed on page 89) in relation to the warm front and the tropopause. E is the temperature transition zone between warm and cold air.

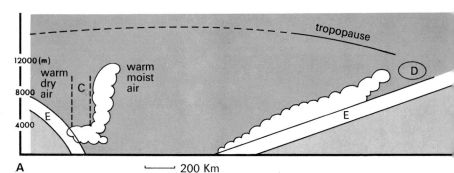

The teleprinter room of a typical national meteorological office. Each weather station is served by a teleprinter and the information, numerically coded as shown on page 35, is received at regular intervals.

To do this a meteorological communications network has been set up throughout the world. The necessary international co-operation is fostered by the World Meteorological Organization, but the actual facilities are provided by the national meteorological services. The observations of the weather are translated into an international numerical code and transmitted to each national meteorological center by teleprinter. For many years these systems were purely national, but teleprinter signals are now transmitted by radio, so that information can be made available to all countries. This means that the forecaster receives information from a large area, and sufficiently quickly to be of use. The amount of information is large and continues to grow. The British Meteorological Office receives about 2 million coded figures daily and the figure is increasing at the rate of 6 per cent per annum. To avoid "meteorological indigestion," automated methods—discussed later in this chapter—are now being used.

The first essential for weather analysis is to construct an adequate three-dimensional picture of the atmosphere. As this changes constantly, new pictures have to be drawn at regular intervals. The most practicable way to prepare such a three-dimensional picture is by the construction of maps of the various weather elements for different levels of the atmosphere. There are, of course, an infinite number of possible levels in the atmosphere for which a chart could be drawn, and the selected levels are the result of a compromise between the meteorologist's desire for the fullest possible picture and the time available for analysis before a forecast must be made. The basic surface and upper-air charts are supplemented by upper-air soundings and cross-section analyses.

Weather Charts

The World Meteorological Organization, realizing some time ago the importance of securing uniformity of procedures throughout the world, instructed the Commission for Synoptic Meteorology to issue a guide to the preparation of synoptic weather charts and diagrams, which would include specifications of base maps as well as plotting techniques. This guide has recently been completed. Three projections are to be used for base maps: the stereographic projection for the polar areas with standard parallel of latitude $60°$; Lambert's conformal conic projection for middle latitudes, with standard parallels of $10°$ and $40°$, or $30°$ and $60°$; and Mercator's projection for the equatorial regions, with true scale at standard parallel of latitude $22\frac{1}{2}°$. Scales of maps are also suggested, the largest of which is $1:3,000,000$; this is employed by the British Meteorological Office to follow atmospheric conditions over the British Isles at hourly intervals. Nearly all these maps are printed with brown or ocher coloring for the frame, title, scale, grid, and contour lines for surface and upper-air maps, and blue for water areas and rivers. Diagrams that are essential to the analysis of thermal, humidity, and wind structure in the vertical are described later in this chapter.

Surface and upper-air observations are plotted on these standard maps by means of letters, figures, and symbols arranged around the point of observation in fixed positions in the form of a *plotting model*. The recommended surface plotting model is shown on page 68. There are many others but the one presented here is among the most basic and serves to remind us of the tremendous amount of information that may be displayed around one such model. Not all the elements allowed for in the various plotting models are necessarily included in the plot, either because the purpose of the particular chart does not require it or because the information is missing from the report. The plotting model is so designed that a single color, usually black or blue, can be used for plotting, but some services use two colors, the second usually being red.

With the use of such plotting models, the basic data for analysis are put onto the chart. The actual plotting is a chore, especially when it has to be done against the clock. Usually two assistants work simultaneously on one chart and use two-headed pens, one nib for black ink, the other for red. A portion of a chart on which the station information has been plotted is on page 68, together with a fully plotted and analyzed surface chart for the North Atlantic.

Analyzing Surface Charts

What are the steps in the analysis of these surface and upper-air charts? First, there is the identification and marking of special states of the atmosphere or of specific atmospheric processes according to conventional models—usually fronts. Secondly, there is the drawing of *isopleths* (lines connecting points of the same value) of pressure, so that observations made at discrete points provide an overall spatial picture of the pressure field. These two ways of looking at the atmosphere are used very much in conjunction with one another. Usually some sort of model atmospheric system, in cartographic form, is chosen at the outset as a basic guide to the analyst, and the weather element distribution—be it pressure, temperature, or any other—is made to fit into this theoretical pattern.

A consideration of frontal analysis will illustrate this point. The Norwegian team made three main contributions to the techniques of weather analysis. First it was shown that if we accept the ideal cyclone model (see page 64) then a front could be recognized from very few observations. Secondly, the concept of an air mass led to a method of classifying weather conditions according to air mass type. And thirdly, the configuration of fronts was related to the life cycle of the ideal

T_gT_g	T_eT_e	C_h	E_s	
	TT	C_m	PPP	
VV	ww	(N)	pp	a
	T_dT_d	$C_{l\ h}N_h$	W	R_t
	T_sT_s T_wT_w	d_wd_w $P_w\ H_w$	RR D_sV_s	

Surface and upper-air observations are plotted on standard maps by means of letters, figures, and symbols arranged around the point of observation in fixed positions; the surface model is shown above. The elements are keyed at right. Below: portion of surface chart on which observations have been plotted in this way.

N	Fraction of celestial dome covered by cloud (in eighths)
dd	Direction of surface wind (an arrow from appropriate direction)
ff	Speed of surface wind (represented by barbs)
VV	Visibility
WW	Present weather (100 symbols)
W	Past weather (9 symbols)
PPP	Atmospheric pressure
TT	Air temperature
C_L, C_M, C_H	Types of cloud (27 symbols)
N_h	Fraction of celestial dome covered by all C_L cloud(s) present, and, no C_L present, that fraction covered by all C_M cloud(s) present
h	Height, above ground, of the base of the lowest cloud seen
T_dT_d	Dew-point temperature
a	Characteristic of pressure change
PP	Pressure change
D_sV_s	Direction and speed of movement of ship
T_sT_s	Difference between air temperature and sea temperature
T_wT_w	Temperature of sea
d_wd_w	Direction of movement of the waves
P_w	Period of the waves
H_w	Height of the waves
RR	Amount of precipitation
R_t	Time at which precipitation began or ended
T_eT_e	Extreme temperatures
T_gT_g	Grass minimum temperatures
E	State of the ground
S	Depth of snow

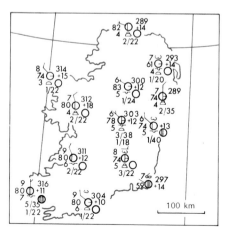

Right: an assistant plots observations on a chart in preparation for analysis. Below: analyzed surface chart for North Atlantic area, with observations plotted, pressure isopleths (isobars) drawn in, and fronts identified.

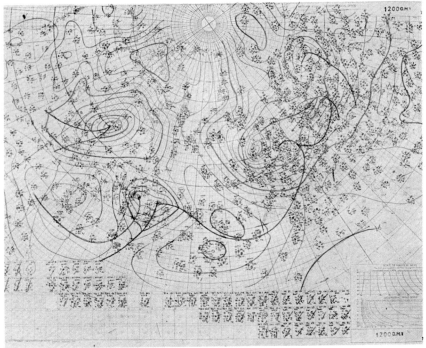

cyclone. Frontal analysis, however, has now somewhat lost its value, because in well-observed areas, for example over land, a picture of rain belts and other weather associated with fronts can be built up more easily and completely from observations than by using any model front. Forecasters are indeed more interested in differences between each individual front and the model than with the ideal front itself. But despite these disadvantages, the operational routine of most midlatitude meteorological services still includes delineation of fronts as one of the first basic steps of surface chart analysis.

There are six main types of front: warm, cold, occlusion, back-bent occlusion, secondary cold, quasi-stationary: and warm and cold front waves. All these are descriptions of the state at any one time of the general polar front, which is considered to form the transition zone between tropical and polar air masses. Their names are closely related to the evolution of the model depression as outlined by the Norwegians.

It is very difficult to define a front exactly, and the requirements of forecasting have led to rather drastic modifications of the original ideas. Meteorologists usually define the ideal frontal surface as a discontinuity of density through a deep layer of the troposphere, but this definition has become blurred by the practicalities of forecasting. Clouds and precipitation, and many linear weather forms, have been incorrectly labeled as fronts. Other modifications are also made. For example, though the temptation to join up boundaries of rain areas with a line must be resisted, air-mass boundaries based on changes in dew point and cloud amount and type may be usefully marked with frontal symbols. Purists may object but in operational forecasting almost anything is justified by expediency.

Many authors have written on the intricacies of frontal analysis, but most of them have concentrated on the actual mechanics of fronts rather than their routine identification, which concerns us here. The first step in frontal analysis of the surface chart is to look at previous charts to build up a sense of continuity in the movement of atmospheric systems. The next step is to look at the newly plotted observations for changes in values. Temperature, dew point, and wind field are the three

Weather Element	Observations in warm air	Observations in cold air
Pressure	Does not identify directly although a trough in the pattern may assist the identification	Does not identify directly although a trough in the pattern may assist the identification
Air temperature	Warmer behind the front	Colder ahead of the front
Sea minus air temperature	Less behind the front	Greater ahead of the front
Wind direction	Blows from a point several degrees veered from the wind in the cold air	Blows from a point several degrees backed from the wind in the warm air
Dew Point	Higher in the warm air	Lower in the cold air
Dew point depression	Often less than in the cold air	Often greater than in the warm air; except in precipitation, when it may be about the same as or even less than in the warm air
Pressure tendency	Falls less sharply than in the cold air; occasionally rises slowly	Falls, or falls more sharply than in warm air
Weather	Overcast sky, except inland in summer; occasionally rain and particularly drizzle, which may be heavy on coasts exposed to wind; fog on exposed coasts and covering hills	Usually continuous rain or snow, but sometimes only light and intermittent; occasionally no weather, particularly inland in summer
Cloud amount	Usually 8/8 low cloud but sometimes broken low cloud inland in summer	8/8 low cloud in precipitation occasionally only broken low cloud inland in summer; usually 8/8 medium and high cloud
Cloud type	Stratiform clouds	High, medium and stratiform clouds, nimbostratus in precipitation
Visibility	Often good but poor on coasts exposed to the wind, and elsewhere in drizzle and fog	Often good but poor in precipitation

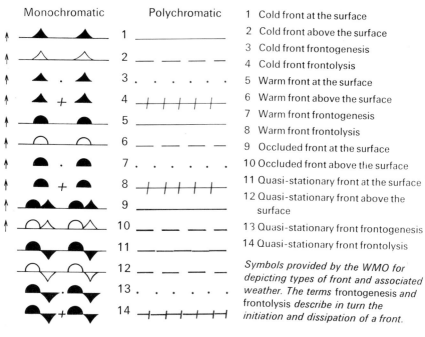

Monochromatic		Polychromatic	

1 Cold front at the surface
2 Cold front above the surface
3 Cold front frontogenesis
4 Cold front frontolysis
5 Warm front at the surface
6 Warm front above the surface
7 Warm front frontogenesis
8 Warm front frontolysis
9 Occluded front at the surface
10 Occluded front above the surface
11 Quasi-stationary front at the surface
12 Quasi-stationary front above the surface
13 Quasi-stationary front frontogenesis
14 Quasi-stationary front frontolysis

Symbols provided by the WMO for depicting types of front and associated weather. The terms frontogenesis *and* frontolysis *describe in turn the initiation and dissipation of a front.*

most useful parameters, but all observations help. The table on page 71 gives a check list for the identification of a warm front: a similar one exists for cold fronts. This check list is a guide to only the more elementary frontal characteristics. There is no substitute for experience, however, and only familiarity with plotted charts can give the analyst real insight into these transitional zones.

Finally, having considered all the relevant information and possible explanations for apparent observational anomalies—*diurnal* variations, for instance (that is, variations through the course of the day)—the analyst may decide to draw in a front. Very often it will be one of the eight types mentioned earlier, but the World Meteorological Organization recognizes, and provides symbols for, numerous front and associated phenomena, shown on this page. The terms *frontogenesis* and *frontolysis* refer in turn to the initiation and dissipation of a frontal zone; an *instability line* is any nonfrontal line or band of convective

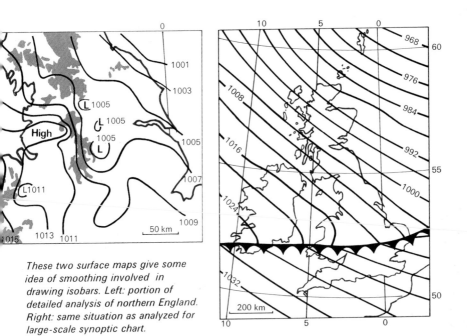

These two surface maps give some idea of smoothing involved in drawing isobars. Left: portion of detailed analysis of northern England. Right: same situation as analyzed for large-scale synoptic chart.

activity in the atmosphere; and a *shear line* is a narrow zone or line across which there is an abrupt change in the horizontal wind parallel to this line.

Once the major frontal systems have been identified, the analyst usually turns to the observations of pressure, the values of which are reduced to mean sea level. The analysis consists of drawing isopleths so that the distribution of pressure (the *pressure field*) appears as a continuous surface. Even within such a simple procedure, it is possible to construct radically different pictures of the pressure pattern for the same data. If observations are all given equal weight and the isobar interval is small enough, a quite complicated mesoscale picture may emerge. On the synoptic scale it is usual to apply smoothing to the observations so as to describe only the major disturbances of the troposphere and form a suitable basis for forecasting. The difference between the two charts on this page gives some indication of the smoothing involved. In routine pressure-field analysis, *isobars* (lines joining equal values of pressure) are usually drawn at 4-mb. intervals, although 5 mb. is acceptable to the World Meteorological Organization. Depending on the scale and purpose of the map, multiples or submultiples of these basic intervals are used. Whatever the intervals, the 1000-mb. isobar is always included.

Analysis of the pressure field serves two main purposes. First it allows the identification of pressure systems that are often, though not always, associated with a particular type of weather. Secondly, in the middle latitudes it is possible, by using the geostrophic balance, to construct a picture of the wind field from a study of the pressure distribution.

The *geostrophic balance* is diagramed on page 81. It is in fact the balance between two influences upon a wind—the pull down the pressure gradient into the center of a depression, which is counterbalanced by the *Coriolis* or geostrophic force— that is, the influence on the wind of the earth's rotation, which causes the wind to swerve in the Northern Hemisphere to the right, and in the Southern Hemisphere to the left. It is this effect

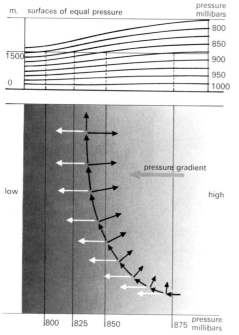

The knowledge that winds tend to blow along rather than across isobars is a most useful tool in weather analysis. Top left shows a sectional view of pressure gradient in isobaric surfaces from 1000 mb. to 800 mb. Below left shows the development of the geostrophic wind at the 1500-m. level. The pressure gradient force is represented by the white arrows, and this induces winds (shown by black arrows) from the 875-mb. lines. As soon as the wind blows, the Coriolis force (blue arrows) begins to deflect it to the right (in Northern Hemisphere) and continues to increase as wind speed increases until balance is achieved with the wind blowing parallel to the isobars.

of the earth's spin (greatest at the poles, zero at the equator) that prevents winds from blowing directly to the center of a depression and makes them travel around it. Where the Coriolis force and the pressure gradient force are equal, in the situation known as *geostrophic balance,* the wind in the free atmosphere blows along the isobars.

The use of pressure system models and the wind field have been powerful tools in midlatitude forecasting for most of this century, and will probably continue to play an important role. In equatorial areas, however, the relationship between pressure and wind is not as simple as in midlatitudes. As the Coriolis force tends toward zero as one approaches the equator, little or no geostrophic balance exists. In such areas it is therefore necessary to analyze the wind field directly from surface and upper-air observations.

The description of fronts and the pressure field form the basis of surface chart analysis, but many parameters that are plotted around the station model are not used in this technique. Surface temperatures and humidities, cloud types, amounts, and heights, surface winds, and visibilities are left as plotted spot observations that are integrated mentally by the analyst. The resulting surface chart provides a picture of many factors, some applying to the surface layers proper, some (e.g. cloud types and heights) applying to the free atmosphere at any level of the troposphere, some represented as continuous fields, some left as spot values—the whole forming a fine tool in the hands of the expert.

The Value of Radar Information

The routine use of radar and satellites means that clouds and rain areas can be drawn in quite accurately on a fairly large scale. As much of the weather we experience is associated with clouds, these comparatively new observational techniques, which can partly overcome the previous problems of depicting local and diurnal variation of cloudiness, allow a direct analysis of weather-producing features rather than intelligent guesswork from models constructed from other parameters or from surface observation. The difference between the two approaches is illustrated on pages 76 and 78. The chart produced by the

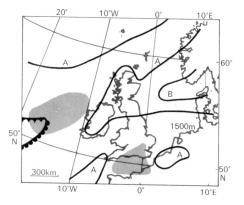

Maps on this page show value of satellite information in cloud analysis. Left: typical cloud analysis from surface observations. Line A indicates limit of middle cloud, B limit of cirrus cloud. Below: chart of same situation using TIROS operational cloud analysis. Note how satellite provides detailed picture of cloud in poorly served ocean area.

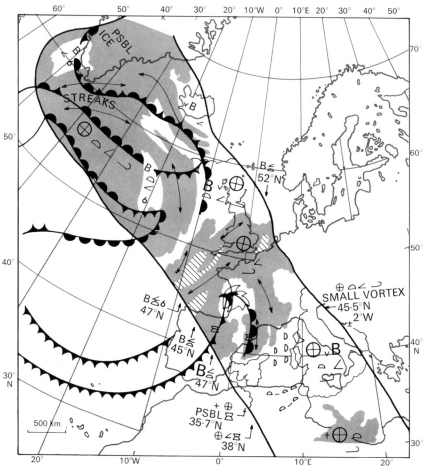

Right: receiving a satellite cloud
analysis by facsimile transmitter.
Below: section of radar summary
cloud map of the United States as
received by facsimile. This map is
built up from coded reports from all
weather radar stations; reports are
overlapped to reduce errors due to
beam attenuation. Arrows indicate
echo movement during past hour, NE
means "no echoes reported," NR "no
report," and so on. There is still,
however, a dangerous degree of
subjectivity in the system.

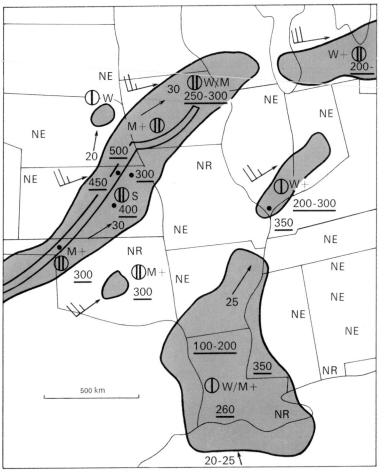

most commonly employed type of "nephanalysis" involves the colored shading on the normal working charts of areas of precipitation or fog as observed on the ground or the marking of the edge of a stratus or stratocumulus sheet with a colored line. The use of radar and satellite information allows a far more detailed picture to be drawn.

There are, however, a number of difficulties in the use of radar. Often the method of display means that the information is transient in nature, and unless a photograph is taken or a detailed description is made of the radarscope, there is no permanent record of the echo distribution. A second limitation is that the plan position indicator (PPI) presentation of a single radar is of little value in outlining rain areas on a synoptic scale. It is, however, possible to use radar coverage in weather analysis, as is done on a routine basis in the United States.

The dense weather radar network in the United States, shown on page 45, is composed primarily of Weather Bureau (now ESSA) sets. In 1963 there were 97 radars of different types in the Bureau network. Observations taken at hourly intervals are encoded in a style called "abbreviated plain language" and transmitted to a convenient center at Kansas City. Information in the observations includes the location, movement, intensity,

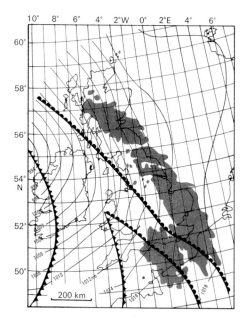

Map shows clearly the value of radar information in building up an accurate picture of rain areas. The area of precipitation here is further ahead of the surface warm front than would normally be expected.

intensity change, vertical development of isolated cells, and echo coverage for echoes in the form of bands, lines, or areas. The message is in fact a description of the radar display, and the quality of the description varies with the complexity of the echo pattern, the scale of the elements in the patterns, the time available to make and encode the observations, and the judgement of the observer. At the central office, these hourly observations from different stations are used to prepare both a summary of the weather in abbreviated plain language and a map showing radar weather information for the entire country. The map is constructed by the simple overlapping of reports in an effort to reduce errors due to attenuation of the radar beams. An example of this type of analysis is shown on page 77. There is obviously a large degree of subjectivity in this procedure and it is hoped that a standard-format digitized code, as illustrated on page 40, will eliminate this source of error and in addition lend itself to modern computer techniques of data processing.

Operational analysis of this kind, like most radar research into synoptic rainfall patterns, has been done only in the United States. Many discrepancies between distributions observed by radar and those predicted by synoptic models have been found and one such, discovered by British researchers, is illustrated opposite. This was constructed on the same principles as the routine analysis, but it provides a research problem rather than the basis for a forecast.

Before considering the role of satellites in weather analysis it is important to complete our review of the more conventional, well-tried methods of analysis, for most meteorologists maintain that the use of satellite observations should complement, rather than replace, analysis based on available conventional data. First, therefore, let us take a look at the routine analysis of upper-air charts and soundings, and other methods such as cross-sectional and frontal contour analysis.

Analyzing Upper-Air Charts and Diagrams
    Upper-air charts give the necessary third dimension to our picture of the atmosphere. The plotting model is of a similar pattern to that used for surface observations and, as with surface

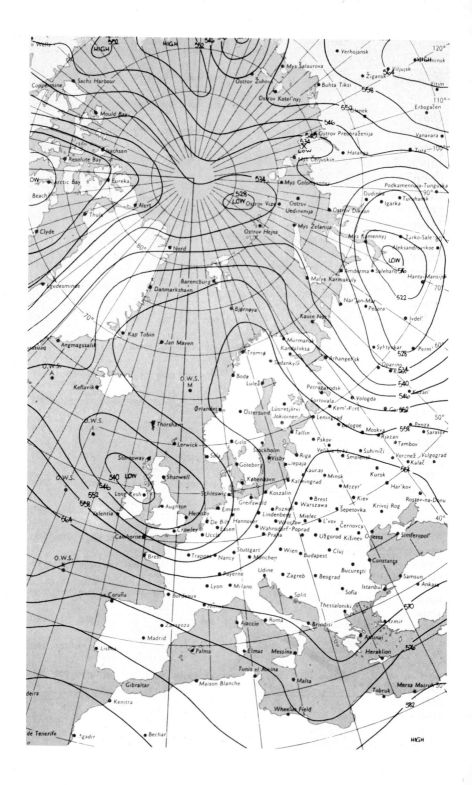

charts, the aim of the analysis is first to draw isopleths to describe a meteorological field. It has always been standard practice to plot the pressure distribution, but the ways in which this is done have varied over the past few decades. The first attempted method appeared to be the most logical one at the time; it involved the construction of pressure charts for certain heights (1 km., 3 km., 6 km., or 3000 ft., 10,000 ft., 20,000 ft.). More recently, this technique has been superseded in all countries by plotting the height of pressure *(isobaric)* surfaces to give *contour charts*. The World Meteorological Organization recommends the following standard isobaric surfaces: 1000, 850, 700, 500, 400, 300, 200, 150, 100, 70, 50, 30, 20, and 10 mb. It also suggests that national services should provide charts for at least four of five standard isobaric surfaces—850, 700, 500, 300, and 200 mb.—so that the three-dimensional picture of the pressure distribution should be as complete as possible.

This system of plotting pressure values may, at first sight, seem unnecessarily complicated. There are two main reasons for doing it in this way. First, it allows the use of one geostrophic wind scale for all levels, the relationship between the geostrophic wind speed and the contour pattern being independent of density. The scale itself is based upon a measure of the contour gradient and may be printed on the standard upper-air chart or engraved on a transparent base. In the former case, dividers are used to step off the intervals along the normals between

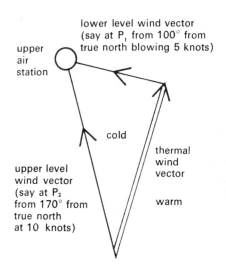

Left: part of an upper-air chart on which the 500-mb. isobaric surface has been plotted. Right: diagram illustrates concept of thermal wind as described in text. If we know magnitude and direction of wind at two levels, by joining end of upper wind vector (line representing direction and, by length, magnitude or speed of wind) to end of lower wind vector we automatically draw in magnitude and direction of thermal wind. Because (in Northern Hemisphere) thermal wind has cold air at left and warm air at right, this establishes location of masses of relatively warm and cold air.

upper air station

lower level wind vector (say at P_1 from 100° from true north blowing 5 knots)

cold

upper level wind vector (say at P_2 from 170° from true north at 10 knots)

thermal wind vector

warm

neighboring contours; in the latter the scale is placed on the chart at right angles to the contours with the base line of the scale in contact with one of the isopleths. The second advantage of isobaric charts is the fact that the same geostrophic scale can be applied to a thickness chart giving circulation and thermal characteristics of the atmosphere at any one time. Whereas contour charts show us the circulation at the level for which they are drawn, *thickness charts* implicitly give us the temperature distribution throughout any defined layer—usually the 1000–500 mb. layer—because the thickness of any layer is directly proportional to the mean temperature of the air in the layer. But to investigate more fully the variations of temperature, wind, and humidity in the vertical, it is necessary to analyze the radiosonde observations.

The thermal, humidity, and wind properties of the atmosphere, as sampled by an upper-air station at 12-hourly intervals, are illustrated in two distinct ways, on two different forms of chart: these are the hodograph and the tephigram, which we shall now look at in turn.

The *hodograph* (see opposite) is essentially a drawing of a protractor with concentric circles at specified distances (representing speeds) from the central point. The winds at different pressure levels are drawn as *vectors* (lines of appropriate length and direction) from the origin and give an immediate indication of the nature of change of wind direction and speed with height. With this basic information we can make deductions about the distribution of relatively cold and warm air and about the advection of air at different temperatures at upper levels. These deductions are possible because of the concept of the *thermal*

Opposite: the hodograph allows illustration of variation with height of wind speed and direction. From this, using the thermal wind concept, we can make certain deductions about the distribution of relatively warm and cold air. The diagram shows the wind data (top), the hodograph plot and analysis (center), and the inferences (bottom). Two processes are illustrated: first the simple plotting of wind direction and speed and labeling with each level, e.g. at 400 mb. the wind was from 140° at 67 knots; secondly, the drawing of thermal wind arrows in each layer by joining the plotted dots. From this we can see, for instance, that in the 700–600 mb. layer the thermal wind arrow is orientated roughly NW–SE, so that relatively warm air must be to its right (i.e. NE) and relatively cold air to its left (i.e. SW).

Level (mb)	surface	900	850	800	700	600	500	400	300
Direction	150	140	150	160	140	130	140	140	130
Speed	05	18	20	19	13	32	47	67	87

(Direction in degrees from true north. Speed in Knots).

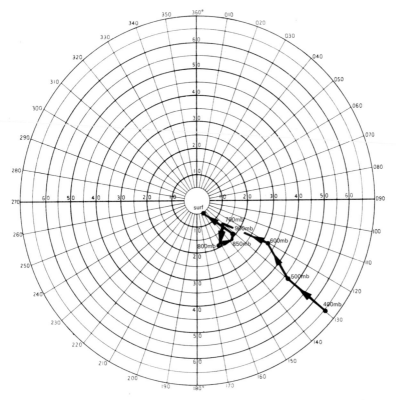

Layer	Warm	Cold
Surface-900 mb	NE	SW
900-850 mb	ESE	WNW
850-800 mb	SSE	NNW
800-700 mb	WNW	ESE
700-600 mb	NE	SW
600-500 mb	ENE	WSW
500-400 mb	NE	SW

wind and it is worth digressing a little to explain this idea.

Consider two levels in the atmosphere, p_1 and p_2. At level p_1 there is no pressure gradient and consequently no wind. In the layer between the two levels p_1 and p_2 there is a temperature gradient. In the warmer part of the layer the vertical pressure gradient is less than in the cooler part and this results in a pressure gradient and associated wind at the level p_2. This wind is thus caused by the thermal characteristics of the layer in question and is called the *thermal wind*. It blows along the gradient of mean temperature in the layer, with colder air to its left in the Northern Hemisphere. The situation we have just outlined is rather hypothetical in that there was no wind at level p_1, but it does illustrate the principle involved: that the wind vector at the higher level is equal to that at the lower level plus the effect of the thermal field, i.e. the thermal wind. The diagram on page 81 illustrates this effect. We can see that if we know the magnitude and direction of the wind at two levels in the atmosphere, by joining the end of the upper wind vector to the end of the lower wind vector we automatically draw in the magnitude and direction of the thermal wind. Because we know that (in the Northern Hemisphere) the thermal wind has cold air to its left and warm air to its right, we can discover the location of masses of relatively cold and warm air.

The hodograph, therefore, is a diagram that makes it possible to identify the thermal wind easily. The example on page 83 is a typical case. The table gives the direction and speed of the wind at different pressure levels above the surface station: the hodograph is constructed from this data. The lines drawn on the hodograph represent the thermal winds in the different layers. Except for the 800–700 mb. layer, relatively warm air lies to the east and is being blown toward the station by the wind. This is just one random example of how the analysis of the vertical wind field can tell us something about the changing thermal structure of the atmosphere.

The hodograph is more detailed in its description than the contour and thickness charts, but perhaps not as detailed as the information that can be shown on a thermodynamic diagram called the *tephigram*. This diagram (see opposite) is a network

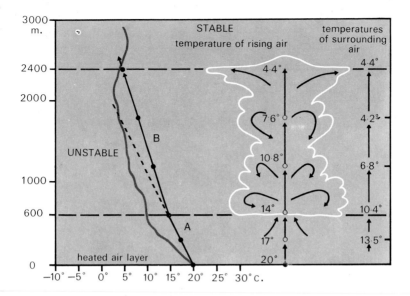

The tephigram is used for analyzing stability in the atmosphere. Above: schematic diagram shows the instability of a parcel of air that rises adiabatically. The blue line represents the temperature drop or lapse in the surrounding atmosphere, line A represents the dry adiabatic lapse rate (see text), and line B the saturated adiabatic lapse rate in a parcel of air that rises under its own buoyancy. The right-hand side shows the temperatures of the parcel and the surrounding atmosphere at certain points, illustrating the relative warmth of the parcel and the cloud that would form above the condensation level. Below: an actual plot on a tephigram, in which thick line AB is equivalent to the blue line above and the thin curved line AB is equivalent to the line B above.

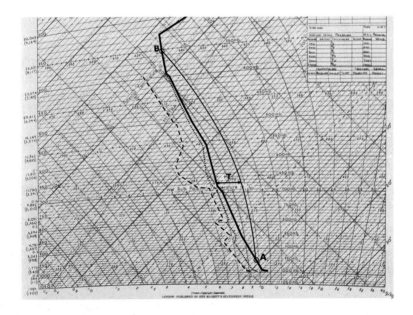

of lines representing the changes with height of five atmospheric parameters: temperature, pressure, humidity, dry bulb potential temperature, and wet bulb potential temperature. When dry bulb and dew-point temperatures from a radiosonde ascent are plotted on this diagram, many useful conclusions can be drawn from an inspection of the resultant curve in the context of the mixing ratio, and dry and wet bulb potential temperature curves. For instance, the distribution of temperature and dew point as portrayed on such a diagram often aids the identification of fronts, if the presence of one is suggested by surface chart analysis. The vertical distribution of wet bulb potential temperature (a parameter that is little affected by evaporation or pressure changes) is a useful guide to air mass recognition. Yet important as these two pieces of information are, it is in the description of the stability of the atmosphere and potential depth of clouds that the thermodynamic diagram is most useful.

Here it is necessary to outline some basics of stability analysis. For initial simplicity, we assume that air rises in discrete thermally insulated parcels, that is, there is no output or input of heat from the parcel to the surrounding atmosphere or vice versa. Such a process is called *adiabatic*. As a non-saturated parcel rises and expands using its internal heat energy, it cools at a constant rate of $1°C$ per 100 m. This fall in temperature is known as the *dry adiabatic lapse rate* and it is represented on the tephigram by the straight lines of constant dry bulb potential temperature, sloping from bottom right to top left. If the parcel is saturated, the adiabatic cooling due to uplift leads to a compensatory release of latent heat from condensed vapor and so the parcel cools at a slower rate than the dry adiabatic. This rate, varying from $0.5°$ to $0.7°C$ per 100 m., is known as the *saturated adiabatic lapse rate* and is represented on the tephigram by the lines of constant wet bulb potential temperature, curving from bottom right to top left.

It is the relationship between the adiabatic lapse rates (component parts of the tephigram) and the lapse of temperature and humidity in the atmosphere (from the radiosonde data) that forms the basis of stability analysis. If the environmental temperature lapse is greater than the dry adiabatic, then any parcel that rises and cools at the dry adiabatic rate will at any time be warmer than the surrounding air. It will move under its own buoyancy and in such a situation the atmosphere is said to be unstable. Conversely, if the environmental lapse rate is less than the dry adiabatic lapse rate, then the same parcel would find itself moving into a cooler environment and would tend to lose its buoyancy and return to its original position. When this happens, the atmosphere is said to be *stable*. The same arguments are true if we consider the path of a saturated parcel along a saturated adiabatic line in relation to the environmental temperature curve, as shown in the diagram on page 85.

This very brief sketch of stability analysis is a necessary preamble to the following example, which illustrates the use of the tephigram. In the tephigram on page 85 the dry bulb and dewpoint temperatures are plotted directly from the radiosonde data, but the wet bulb temperatures are derived from them. The sounding was taken in conditions favorable for thunderstorms, and as such well illustrates how the tephigram describes stability conditions in the atmosphere. If a parcel of air were to rise adiabatically from the surface layers of the atmosphere, it would become saturated and, in this particular case, buoyant relative to the surrounding air at point A. From point A (at 950 mb.) to point B (at 350 mb.) the parcel would cool at approximately the saturated adiabatic rate. Throughout this deep layer of the atmosphere, it would move upward under its own buoyancy. As the layer in question was about 8000 meters deep, it is not surprising that thunderstorms broke out on this particular day. The assumption that parcels of air are warmed or cooled adiabatically is a remarkably accurate approximation to reality, and in this particular case suggests that at one level the in-cloud air was about 4°C (T) warmer than the air around it and the energy available to the rising parcel (directly proportional to the shaded area on the diagram) was very large.

Cross-section and Frontal Contour Analysis

Vertical cross sections are rarely used on a routine basis because they take so long to prepare, but they are useful in clarifying the vertical structure of such phenomena as fronts and wind maximums. A typical cross-section is diagramed on this page. The line of section is taken near to as many upper-air stations as possible, in such a position that the system under examination is intersected in the most profitable manner. The upper-air stations are plotted out on the horizontal axis and the information for the vertical axis is taken from a thermo-dynamic diagram. The data are then inspected for the existence of fronts and any such features are drawn in, following the same routine as for the surface chart. Temperatures and potential temperatures may then be added. Humidity is usually expressed in the form of dew-point depression or mixing ratios, and wind is represented by lines of constant wind speed *(isotachs)*

Cross sections are useful for clarifying the structure of certain atmospheric systems. Diagram shows variation of temperature with height, a frontal zone, and the tropopause along a line from Thorshavn (Iceland) to Nîmes (France). The broken lines are the limits of a frontal zone; the thick black line is the tropopause and the blue lines are isotherms (lines joining equal values of temperature) at 10°C intervals. The stations at the foot of the diagram are regular upper-air stations (see map on page 80). The analysis is based on temperature values for each pressure level above each station plotted along the vertical lines.

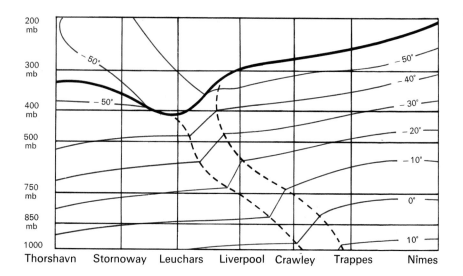

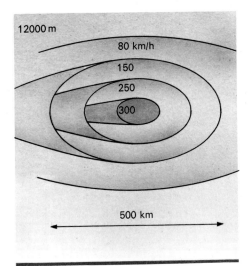

Jet streams meander around the globe like large rivers of rapidly moving air near the tropopause. This schematic diagram of a jet-stream structure shows the variation of wind speeds and the characteristic width of the feature. The vertical axis is much exaggerated, as the depth is often as little as 5 km.

perpendicular to the plane of the section: for clarity the analyses of wind and humidity are often drawn on separate charts.

Frontal contour charts, unlike vertical cross sections, have become routine and are much used by Canadian forecasters for day-to-day weather analysis. This technique simply involves drawing a contour map of a frontal surface, using pressure as the vertical coordinate. This is achieved by tracing the intersection of the upper surface of the frontal zone with the various standard pressure levels and putting the resultant lines on one map. Such a procedure requires the careful identification of frontal zones on aerological diagrams and is often aided by a study of the wind field as illustrated on a hodograph. Frontal contour charts have not been used to any extent in the United Kingdom, where the thickness charts are considered an adequate approximation to the frontal contour chart.

The Value of Satellite Information

Surface and upper-air charts together provide the forecaster with the major synoptic features he requires. The value to him of satellite photographs lies in the greater accuracy they give to his picture of atmospheric—and in particular cloud—conditions. Photographs of this kind may be analyzed in two ways: by making nephanalyses of the photograph, such as those on pages 90–91; or by interpreting the photographs themselves, taken and viewed in sequence. With the increasing num-

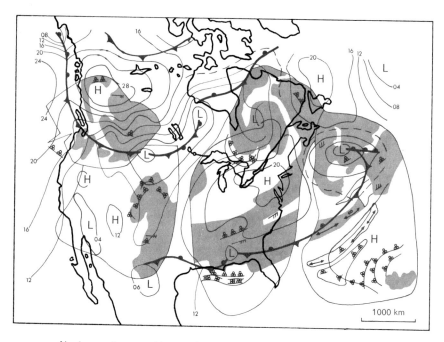

Neph mosaics can either confirm or contradict conventional analyses. Above: the shaded areas representing clouds on neph mosaics have been superimposed on a conventional surface analysis. The cloud structure of the various pressure systems is well illustrated, for instance in the depression to the east of Nova Scotia and in the high-pressure area over Arizona, which is seen to be cloud-free.

ber of pictures available from satellites in a given period of time, this direct analysis of photographs is rapidly gaining ground, though both methods are still used, often side by side.

How valuable are these photographs, taken from approximately 800 km. up, in depicting cloud formations and types? Of the 10 types of cloud listed in the WMO cloud-classification system, only three broad categories are identifiable with the degree of camera resolution, and therefore detail, now obtainable—cumuliform, stratiform, and cirriform. Identification depends upon six main features: brightness, pattern, structure, texture, shape, and size. Most of these are self-evident, but of those that perhaps are not, *structure* refers to the relative height

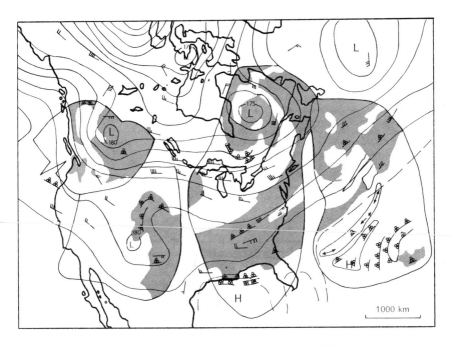

Above: the same nephanalysis superimposed on the appropriate 500-mb. chart. Oddities appear: for instance, the cloud-free area in the well-developed low over Labrador. Also the cloud patterns show no evidence for the closed low at this level over New Mexico.

of visible clouds, and *texture* to the degree of apparent smoothness of cloud surface. Despite all limitations, two new patterns of cloud—*cellular* and *banded*—were soon recognized on the early pictures, and their reality has been subsequently confirmed. They are illustrated on page 24. The cellular pattern usually, but not always, comprises cumuliform clouds and has posed many new problems to meteorologists, particularly because it frequently occurs over oceanic areas where there is no obvious explanation for it. A number of variations exist in the density of the cellular mesh, and the analyst can at present do little more than describe them and their distribution without giving an adequate explanation. Banded patterns occur on many scales

New methods of observation provide new ways of looking at familiar atmospheric systems. *Left:* an original satellite photograph of an occluding depression with its center to the southwest of Iceland. The vortex cloud pattern is well illustrated. *Right:* the nephanalysis constructed from this satellite picture. Note the detailed information that can be abstracted from the photograph. *Below:* the actual analyzed surface chart two hours after satellite picture and nephanalysis were received provides a third, conventional view of the same depression.

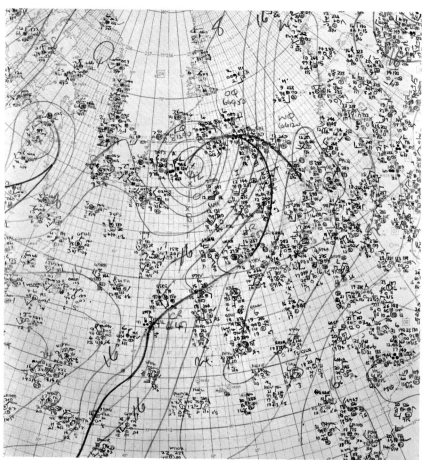

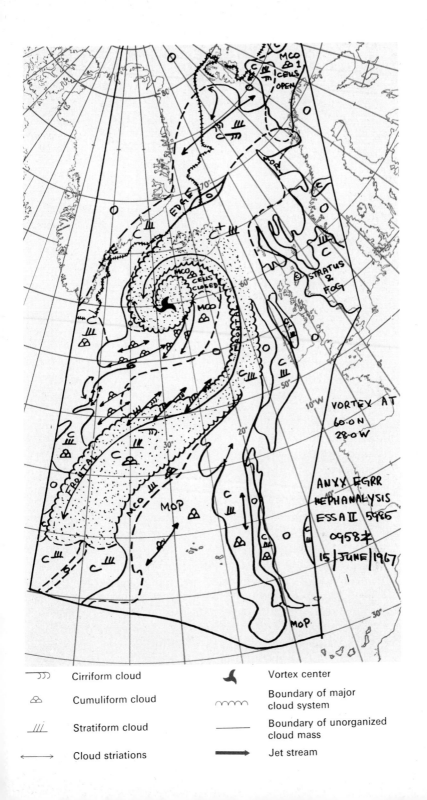

	Cirriform cloud		Vortex center
	Cumuliform cloud		Boundary of major cloud system
	Stratiform cloud		Boundary of unorganized cloud mass
	Cloud striations		Jet stream

ranging from cloud *streets*, or linear formations, a few miles
long to the linear organization of cloud along a front several
hundred miles wide. All these are now directly observable by
satellite. Most of the clouds in banded patterns are also of the
cumuliform type, but other types, such as mountain lee waves,
are often found.

This kind of analysis is simply concerned with reading cloud
types. The next stage in cloud analysis is to identify on the
photographs the significant synoptic features as expressed in
cloud form. Most of these features are associated with the
cyclonic vortex as illustrated in the sequence of photographs
on page 53. The catherine-wheel-like picture is made up of the
vortex center, with perhaps two fronts spiraling out from it.
Clouds associated with the jet stream can also be recognized:
they are usually of the cirriform kind occurring on the tropical
side of the jet axis, in the form of either an extensive cirrus shield
that ends abruptly along the jet axis, or long narrow bands. The
fronts and vortex center are usually quite unmistakable if the
cyclone is well developed, and are visible as massive banks of
cumuliform cloud, perhaps even cumulonimbi, that are recorded on satellite photographs. There are an infinite number of
stages in the life cycle of such an atmospheric system, and more
and more of these stages are now being recorded on film by
satellite. This allows the analyst to build up a library (real or
mental) of synoptic developments in terms of actual cloud
forms, with a consequent improvement in overall analysis.

Although the methods of interpretation outlined above form
the core of cloud analysis, the availability of APT pictures has
not made conventional nephanalysis completely obsolete. In
Chapter 2 we noted the first attempt at cartographic representation of cloud patterns, but since that time there has been much
development in the routine methods of cloud analysis. The
procedure falls into two parts—location and classification.

In locating clouds, it is necessary to know the position of
the satellite and the direction of the camera when the picture
was taken. This allows the construction of a *perspective grid*
for the area covered by the picture—an imaginary rectangular
grid on the earth's surface, as it would be seen from the satellite

in a particular position. Obviously many such perspective grids must be prepared for the many altitudes and attitudes taken up by the satellite. If the altitude and nadir angle at which any picture was taken is known, the appropriate grid can be selected and superimposed by projection over the photograph. The significant cloud patterns are then traced on to this grid. These features are transferred to a rectangular grid and then on to a map with a rectangular latitude and longitude lattice. The picture is then fully rectified and in a form that all analysts can understand and use. This method was developed in the *TIROS* orbits and has now been automated. A computer calculates and draws a latitude–longitude grid at the same perspective as the view from the satellite. This grid is superimposed on the photograph and it is then possible to transfer directly on to a normal latitude–longitude map.

Nephanalyses are usually prepared for one photograph, but the scale of analysis is governed chiefly by the size of the area under consideration. For example the British Isles is often covered by one photograph, but analysts in the United States need many photographs to cover the whole country. This has led to the development of "neph mosaics," made by piecing together separate nephanalyses in a manner analogous to aerial photograph mosaics. These are superimposed on conventional surface and 500-mb. analyses, as shown on pages 90–91.

The following quotation gives one example of how this superimposition helps analysis: "Over New Mexico, the conventional 500-mb. analysis indicates a short wave is passing around the south-east side of the closed system. The cloud pattern . . . does not indicate a closed system. . . . A rather wide area of precipitation is occurring with this southern system which might not have been expected using conventional contour or pressure data alone."

An example of single-picture analysis is on page 93, and the key to this diagram explains the international symbols used in nephanalysis. The original APT picture is shown on page 92 and a conventional analysis making use of it is also shown. In these diagrams we have three different ways of describing the same thing—an occluded depression with a marked vortex at its center and waves on associated fronts. The APT picture and resultant nephanalysis illustrate two main features that were incorporated in the conventional analysis. In the first place, the position of the occlusion vortex was to the south of the surface center of the depression as initially analyzed on the synoptic chart; this had important repercussions on the forecast of subsequent speed of movement of this system. The second improvement due to the APT information was in the location of the warm front. Conventional analysis based on the very scarce data over the Atlantic proved rather vague; but the APT picture filled in this gap in observation. This increased accuracy of analysis is by no means an isolated example. The interpretation and use of APT satellite pictures in operational forecasting frequently provides important new insights into the organization of the cloud, and hence the weather-producing systems of a wide variety of synoptic features.

Automated Analysis

We have now covered all the major techniques of weather analysis, from the oldest—the description of the surface pressure field—to the newest—the use of satellite photographs. All of them involve a great deal of both drudgery and subjectivity. The introduction of computers, however, and the steady increase in their capacity and speed has been a great blessing to weather analysts. It is now possible to automate all the mechanics of chart and diagram production outlined in this chapter. Automated analysis is still in its infancy, and different national services have reached different stages in their installation of the necessary equipment. Consequently this account may be a description of future plans for some services and history for others. The three stages of automatic production of analyzed synoptic charts are the processing of the observational data, the plotting of the data, and the drawing of iso-

Automation in analysis has allowed the introduction of objectivity and greater speed. Observations are fed into the computer and analyses may be given as shown at right. Isopleths are then drawn around the patterns of figures.

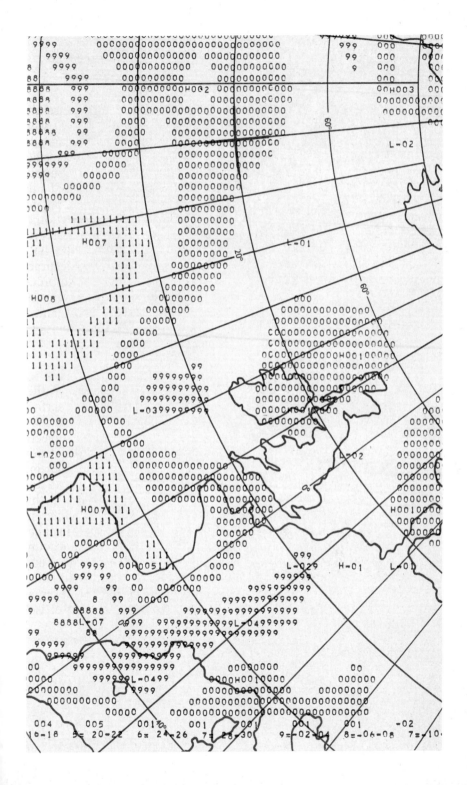

Photograph illustrates the next stage in the process illustrated on page 97. Here the machine has not only analyzed the observations: it is actually drawing in the isopleths to complete the entirely objective analysis.

pleths. Data processing is now a field of such magnitude that for some workers it is an end rather than a means. Its main objectives in meteorology are to receive, decode, check, and store data ready for the second and third stages outlined above. Observations recorded on punched tape are received at a rate of only 7 characters per second per channel, but can be read by the computer at 300–1000 characters per second per channel. Punch cards, punch tape, and magnetic tape and cards are all used for storing data.

The hard labor of plotting the data in the station model format has been eliminated by the use of a machine. Information is fed into the machine from paper tape, magnetic tape, or direct from the computer, and is applied to a simple symbol-generating unit that produces the complete station image as a single short exposure on a piece of microfilm. The microfilm is automatically moved to the appropriate station position while the synoptic information is set up, and overall plotting speeds of two stations per second are normal. Some 300 stations may be exposed on to a single film. The microfilm is then passed through an automatic processing unit and into a standard enlarging printer. The final print is available approximately six minutes after plotting begins and is then ready for analysis, either by hand or by machine. If the isopleth drawing is done by hand, some element of subjectivity is introduced. However, it is now possible to program a computer to analyze the point values quite objectively. This involves calculation of values for the points of intersection of a regular grid from the data of the initial uneven network and provides the basis for machine line-drawing relative to this regular grid. If line-drawing machines are not available, the computer prints out a pattern of digits as shown on page 97. The edges of the shaded areas correspond to the isopleths that the analyst is interested in. This map was constructed in 7 seconds, whereas by hand it would take 30 minutes. Line-drawing equipment requires the cartesian coordinates of many points on a line, and these coordinates are calculated by a computer. Both the British Meteorological Office and the United States Weather Bureau are already using equipment of this kind for routine analysis.

For some years meteorologists have wanted to achieve a completely numerical system of analysis and forecasting. Most of the developments in automation described above were undertaken as first steps toward that objective. As it would be confusing to consider numerical analysis without some understanding of forecasting techniques, we shall postpone that subject until the next chapter.

4 Forecasting

Forecasting has so dominated the field of meteorology for much of this century that to many people the two are synonymous. This impression was probably created during the period leading up to World War II, when most meteorological research had the specific object of improving the quality of forecasts. Although the ultimate aim of today's research is to arrive at a theory of the general atmospheric circulation and thus to achieve accurate long-term prediction, much more research is necessary before even a small improvement in forecasts is achieved. Forecasting crystallizes most of the difficulties that confront meteorologists. Analysis has shown that at any one time in the earth's atmosphere (99 per cent of which lies within 45 km. of the earth's surface) there may be as many as 50 depressions or anticyclones, and 100,000 showers, 2000 of which are thunderstorms. We have seen how these systems are observed and analyzed: what are the techniques used in forecasting their future behavior?

The synoptic method of forecasting—still probably the most widely used—involves much discussion of past, present, and future situations. Here a senior forecaster at ESSA's National Meteorological Center, Suitland, Maryland, leads a daily discussion. Charts behind him on the wall include the surface analysis charts for 6 hours earlier, the current surface analysis, the 500-mb. contour chart for the previous midday, and the 36-hour forecast chart for the 500-mb. surface.

Before 1950 all forecasting followed the synoptic method with little deviation, but since then there have been two important new developments: first, the introduction of numerical methods of analysis and prediction; and secondly, long-range forecasting. Today even this threefold division into synoptic, numerical, and long-range is losing its validity, because numerical techniques are being used increasingly in all types of forecasting. A new threefold division is based on the time periods for which forecasts are made: *short-range* forecasts, usually prepared by synoptic or numerical methods, cover the next 24 hours with a further outlook to 48 or 72 hours ahead; *medium-range* forecasts, again usually prepared by synoptic, or sometimes by numerical methods, are valid for periods up to four days ahead; and *long-range* forecasts, prepared by different methods, are usually made for a month, but the time period can range from anything over five days to a whole season.

In this chapter we shall consider the methods of forecasting under these headings but, before doing so, it is important to stress the close connection between analysis and forecasting on two counts. First, both analysis and forecasting are usually done by the same person—a forecaster who has made himself familiar with the immediate history of the weather situation and who develops a feel for that particular situation. Because of this essential wholeness, the separate treatment of analysis and forecasting in this book, although logical in its sequence, is somewhat artificial.

Secondly, we have seen that the actual process of analyzing a chart is essentially a mental one, except in the case of automated, objective analysis. The same is true of most types of forecast. The prediction is the result of interplay of ideas and procedures in the forecaster's head; it is based on all available evidence, and the manifestation of these ideas and procedures with pencil, paper, and eraser. Consequently, in all but the numerical type of forecast, a description of forecasting techniques does little justice to the insight of the individual synoptic forecaster, something that cannot be represented in the form of words and diagrams.

Short- and Medium-Range Forecasts:
Synoptic Method

Synoptic forecasting is essentially the diagrammatical representation of weather systems through time and the extrapolation of developments of such systems into the future. From the practical point of view, the problem is considered in two parts. First, the forecaster is concerned with the determination of changes in the distribution of such parameters as pressure, pressure tendency, wind, temperature, contour heights and thicknesses—parameters that form the essential framework of a weather system such as a cyclone or anticyclone. Secondly, what has been aptly termed the *fine structure* of weather, in both space and time, must be superimposed on the general synoptic evolution. Fine structure in fact refers to nearly all the weather phenomena that the individual may experience. The familiar showers, fog, thunder, lightning, and sunny periods are all comparatively small on the synoptic scale and occur only against the backcloth of certain synoptic developments.

The whole aim of synoptic forecasting is to work from the present position, as illustrated on the synoptic chart, and to produce a similar chart portraying the circulation at a certain time in the future, usually 24 hours ahead. Once the surface pressure field, frontal positions, and upper-air circulations have been defined, the actual weather is put into the surface chart, using our knowledge of the relationships between synoptic systems and actual weather. This chart, which represents the future surface circulation of the atmosphere, is known as the *prebaratic*. Charts showing the future state of the upper air are called *prontours*.

The oldest, simplest, and one of the most efficient methods of preparing a prebaratic is by extrapolating recent changes into the future. Extrapolation can apply to the movement of systems in space and to their internal development in time. For instance, an anticyclone that has moved 500 km. east in the past 24 hours would be placed 500 km. farther east as the first approximation in a 24-hour prebaratic. Similarly, if the central pressure of the anticyclone had increased from 1020 mb. to 1026 mb. over the past 24 hours, its central pressure would on this basis be forecast to be 1032 mb. on the 24-hour prebaratic. Such extrapolations are helped by observations of thermal gradients on thickness charts and of pressure tendencies at ground level, but they can provide only a skeletal picture of the positions of low- and high-pressure areas. The part played by our knowledge of the dynamics of pressure systems is considered later.

We saw in Chapter 3 that the synoptic model—that is, the ideal synoptic system—is a useful tool in the analysis of weather. The forecaster also makes great use of these models in estimating the likely evolution of the circulation patterns. Despite the many variations in the models of frontal depressions and anticyclones, they are still used as basic forecast techniques. The experienced forecaster soon becomes aware of the misleading simplicity of these textbook diagrams, but there is still the danger that, having a particular model in mind, he will be blind to any alternative possibilities or tendencies.

There is less danger of error in the use of *analogues*. These are synoptic charts of actual past situations that have as much as possible in common with the current situation. If such a chart is found, the evolution of the past situation is studied and the forecast for the current situation follows the same pattern. This system would be an infallible method of forecasting if a perfect analogue could always be found; but in fact, because of the infinite variety of patterns possible in the atmosphere, even reasonably good ones are difficult to find.

Although extrapolation, models, and analogues are all valuable forecasting tools, they are empirical and do not use any general theory of synoptic systems. Most research into forecasting over the past 40 years has been directed at avoiding empiricism and replacing it with some sort of theory. But progress has been very dependent on the availability of data to give a reasonable three-dimensional picture of the atmosphere. With the introduction of aircraft and pilot-balloon soundings in the 1920s, speculations about the behavior of the upper atmosphere could be compared with actuality. It became possible to consider the atmosphere as a dynamic, three-dimensional system rather than as a system that somehow presented the analyst with a surface pressure and frontal distribution. This

Vorticity is extremely useful in synoptic forecasting. It occurs in two basic forms: first, vorticity due to the spin of the earth about its axis (A); and secondly, the relative vorticity of air spinning around a near-vertical axis in depressions and anticyclones in the atmosphere (B). The sum of these two forms is called the absolute vorticity.

"dynamical thinking," and the ability to put some of it into practice, was perhaps the biggest breakthrough in forecasting and meteorology in general. It allowed extrapolation to be modified where necessary and it set the scene for numerical forecasting in the postwar period.

Most of our knowledge of the possible applications of atmospheric dynamics to routine forecasting is due to R. C. Sutcliffe and C. G. Rossby. The frequent occurrence of the former's name in this book gives some idea of the impact he has had on the development of weather forecasting. Both these workers produced, in the 1940s, techniques that are still used in official handbooks on weather forecasting. Sutcliffe was concerned with the evolution of cyclones and anticyclones. Rossby was more interested in the larger tropospheric air currents that meander around the globe, now usually known as *Rossby* or *long waves in the westerlies.*

In order to appreciate Sutcliffe's development theory we need to understand something of the role of vorticity in the atmosphere. Vorticity, which is the measure of the spin of a fluid, has been called the very stuff of the atmosphere. This is readily appreciated when we remember that there are about 50 cyclones and anticyclones spinning in the atmosphere at one time. In meteorology it is useful to consider vorticity in two forms. First, if a mass of air is stationary relative to the earth (i.e. there is no wind), it is still spinning with the earth and, as

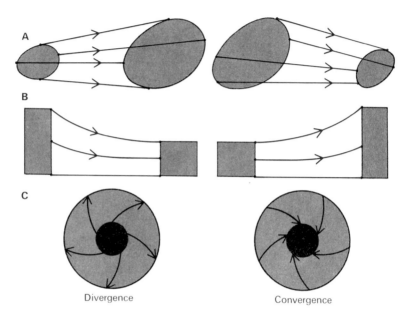

Configuration of divergence and convergence is the essence of dynamic
meteorology and therefore of immense importance in forecasting. Diagrams
illustrate mass divergence (left) and convergence (right) of a parcel of air in
horizontal and vertical planes (A and B). Diagram C demonstrates the change in
vorticity of the air under influence of divergence and convergence.

such, has the same vorticity as the earth. Secondly, if the air
mass rotates with respect to the earth's surface (as in most
weather systems), we have relative vorticity. The sum of these
two vorticities is what an observer from a distant planet would
see, and some meteorologists call this sum of vorticities the
absolute vorticity. The diagram on page 105 illustrates the two
forms of vorticity.

The existence of vorticity in the atmosphere is obvious to
all who study synoptic charts. Similarly, patterns of convergent
and divergent motion soon make themselves evident to the
analyst. It is the configuration of *convergence* and *divergence*
that is the essence of dynamic meteorology and the potentially
valuable tool in forecasting. The vertical motions resulting

from convergence or divergence are the direct cause of much of our weather. It would seem obvious therefore to analyze and forecast divergence (including convergence—i.e. negative divergence) patterns in the atmosphere. Unfortunately this is not possible in the synoptic method because of the method of observing and communicating wind speed and direction. But vorticity and divergence *can* be related to one another by an equation that tells us that changes in the absolute vorticity of a parcel of air arise because of divergence of air motion, and that if divergence is zero the absolute vorticity remains constant.

Using the above relationship as a starting point and making some reasonable assumptions, Sutcliffe arrived at his *development* equation, which tells us that the difference in divergence from one level in the atmosphere to another can be evaluated in terms of the thermal wind (and therefore the mean temperature) in the layer and the difference in relative vorticity at the bounding levels. If, in any area, more air is being extracted at high levels than is being added at low levels (i.e. there is a difference in divergence at the two levels), then the pressure at the low level will fall and upward vertical motion will also occur—this is cyclonic development. The reverse difference of divergence leads to anticyclonic development.

The development equation is important because the parameters necessary for the evaluation of the vorticities at the two levels in the atmosphere and of the thermal wind can be measured from analyzed synoptic charts, particularly contour and thickness charts. Such measurement is a rather lengthy and tedious business and so certain configurations of thicknesses that give rise to particular developments through vorticity changes are presented to the forecaster. These are in fact models and suffer from inconsistencies similar to those in the more familiar synoptic models.

Although Sutcliffe himself admitted that this method was rather crude, it proved to be an enormous step forward in forecasting. At last forecasters had a method that could often suggest how and when extrapolation would fail, when mobile surface systems would be likely to accelerate or stagnate, when and where intensification of the system might occur, and when a track might suddenly curve. Perhaps the greatest omission of the development theory is that it does not predict cyclogenesis in a region of straight, closely packed thickness lines. Although this situation occurs frequently in the atmosphere, on the available charts it is like producing something from nothing. After all, the theory is called "development" and not "initiation."

Rossby's use of the vorticity equation was more ambitious, and the results of his analysis were received with enthusiasm in the early 1950s. Since then, forecasters have grown more dissatisfied with them. It is evident from the vorticity equation that, if there is no divergence, there is no change in the vorticity. The motion is one of constant absolute vorticity. The configuration of divergence overlying convergent air motion, or vice versa, implies a level of no divergent air motion and this level is usually taken as that of the 500-mb. pressure surface (about 5500 m.). On this assumption Rossby showed that very large waves could exist in a broad nondivergent flow at the 500-mb. level in the atmosphere and that their speed of travel depended on their size. Although it is possible to trace these waves in the contour patterns, a fact that makes the technique potentially useful in routine forecasting, the assumptions on which the theory is based are too restrictive for it to be quantitatively useful. The technique is, however, of use in giving some broad indications as to the movement of the wave patterns at 500-mb. Because these waves do to some extent govern the movement of the type of system with which Sutcliffe dealt, the two theories complement one another. It is of course the practicability of the theories on the routine charts that makes them so important.

"Fine Structure" Forecasting Prebaratics, whether prepared by empirical or by mathematical methods, only provide the answer to part of the synoptic forecasting problem as outlined earlier in this chapter. They tell the forecaster what the synoptic circulation will probably be, 24 or more hours ahead, but it still remains to interpret the weather from this type of chart. In this procedure the forecaster can often rely on such well-established physical principles as the laws of radiation and thermodynamics because he is dealing with individual elements. This is in complete contrast to the preparation of a prebaratic, where the forecaster is attempting to foresee the behavior of a system that is a synthesis of many individual meteorological elements. The elements that form the more important synoptic fine structure are clouds and precipitation, wind, temperature, humidity, and visibility. So many techniques for forecasting each element have been devised, often for small specific areas, that it is impossible to list them all. A few examples should serve to indicate the approach of "fine structure" forecasting.

In the United States much effort has gone into developing techniques of forecasting severe local storms such as thunderstorms. The following example is used in forecasting thunderstorms in the Midwest. It is known that storms may form if low-level moist air is capped by a layer of relatively drier air, particularly if the troposphere is *unstable* throughout the greater part of its depth. In this context unstable can be considered to imply that a parcel of air, once forced to move, will continue to move away from its original position, utilizing its own energy. In a stable atmosphere the parcel would tend to return to its original position. This instability can be measured

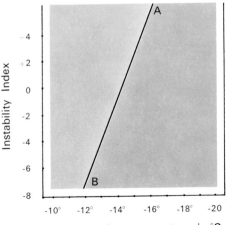

Empirical relationships between meteorological parameters are extremely useful in forecasting "fine structure" phenomena. Diagram shows method of forecasting thunderstorms in midwestern states of USA: vertical axis shows values of instability index taken from thermodynamic diagram such as tephigram. Observed values of this index and the 700-mb. dew-point temperature are plotted: if plot lies to right of line AB thunderstorm is likely; if to left, storm is unlikely.

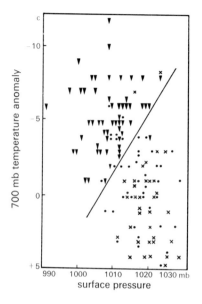

Relationship graph used to forecast shower activity in southeast England. Expected surface pressure is plotted in association with the expected 700-mb. temperature anomaly, or variation from five-day means. Blue line divides diagram into left-hand area containing most of the occasions of widespread showers (triangles) in a given period, and right-hand area containing most occasions of few showers (dots) or no showers (crosses).

in many ways, but most of them use one figure (positive or negative) as an *instability index*. It need not concern us how these indices are arrived at.

Using these basic ideas, it has proved possible to derive an empirical relationship between an instability index and the humidity of the atmosphere at about 3000 m. (actually expressed in terms of the dew-point temperature at the 700-mb. level). As indicated in the diagram on this page, the forecast values of the instability index and the dew points at 700-mb. tell us whether thunderstorms are likely to occur or not.

Techniques of this kind are devised for all weather phenomena. Another example is that between shower activity, surface pressure, and the 700-mb. (3000 m.) temperature *anomaly* (the difference of actual values from mean values) in southeast England. A diagram is plotted of the anomaly (from five-day means) of the temperature at the 700-mb. level against the mean sea-level pressure in the area. For each pair of values of temperature anomaly and pressure a symbol is put onto the diagram: the symbols represent the occurrence of widespread showers, few showers, or no showers (see diagram opposite). The diagram can be divided into two areas as indicated. Of the occasions in one area, 91 per cent were widespread showers; and in the other area, 90 per cent were cases of few or no showers. Thus, as the 700-mb. temperature anomaly and surface pressure can be forecast (as we have seen earlier in this chapter), their forecast values can be read on the axes of this diagram and a prediction of shower activity can be made.

These American and British examples are only two of the many empirical relationships between synoptic features and actual weather. Although these examples may appear specialized to the reader, they are a good indication of the details of weather that fine structure forecasting tries to pinpoint and illustrate. Most national meteorological services are constantly improving old techniques of this type or devising new ones.

In Chapter 3 we saw how useful satellite pictures of clouds were in weather analysis and how an improved analysis usually leads to a better forecast. An example of cloud forms along a front illustrates the latter point. Although cloud forms of this magnitude are hardly synoptic "fine structure" in the generally accepted sense, they are actual "weather" as opposed to what may seem rather abstract circulation prebaratics.

On page 113 we see the usual analysis of a synoptic situation at 1500 GMT on April 8, 1966. This shows a frontal system approaching southwest England and a cold front lying across the Bay of Biscay and close to the Portuguese coast. This front on the 1500 GMT chart was drawn as a logical extrapolation of the position on the 1200 GMT chart in the context of only few ship observations in the Atlantic for 1500 GMT. The forecast chart for 1800 GMT was initially drawn on the basis of both the 1200 GMT and 1500 GMT analyses, but, at the very moment that this forecast chart was being prepared, a TIROS neph-analysis for 1429 GMT was received over the international facsimile network. The cloud analysis strongly suggested that the position of the cold front on the conventionally analyzed 1500 GMT chart was in error. In fact the cold front was shown to be somewhat further east in its southern portion than the routine surface and upper-air observations suggested and, more important, there was a fairly well developed wave on the cold front in the Bay of Biscay nearer to the British Isles than indicated on the original drawing of the 1500 GMT chart (see opposite). This revised 1500 GMT analysis was found to conform well with the 1800 GMT observations when they started to arrive and the amended analysis was used in the preparation of the surface forecast for 1800 GMT on April 9.

On a smaller scale than the above example, it is possible, with the aid of radar pictures, to extrapolate the development of showers or thunderstorms over a period of about six hours. Any longer period would be risky because of the rapid evolution of small precipitating systems. For a slightly longer period, the tephigram is perhaps the most useful tool for cloud and precipitation forecasting. The many possible analyses of the tephigram must always be done within the context of the general synoptic development so that the forecaster can use his estimates of horizontal movement and development effects to forecast the modifications to temperature and humidity characteristics in the vertical. The prognostic sounding is then analyzed to give cloud base, depth, and tops and, with the use of some basic cloud physics, to attempt to determine whether or not precipitation will occur. There are many variations on this theme and all benefit from research into the microphysics of precipitation, and investigations of cloud dynamics.

Although no consideration has been given to the forecasting of wind, temperature, humidity, and visibility, it is hoped that the reader has gained some appreciation of fine structure forecasting, as well as some insight into the whole synoptic method of weather forecasting. For the greater part of its history, forecasting has been considered by its practitioners to be an art. This was primarily due to the lack of data, particularly in the period before World War II. One cannot but admire the sheer skill of those forecasters who, by long experience and careful judgment, produced forecasts only slightly inferior to those of today. However the whole synoptic method makes no contribution at all to prediction by methods of exact calculation. It is to these methods that we now turn.

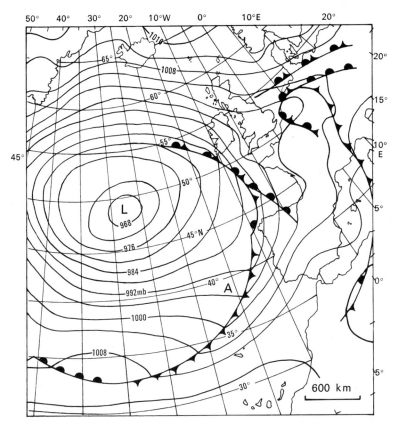

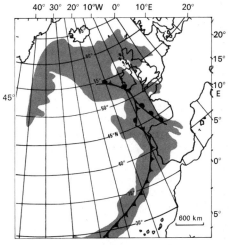

Maps demonstrate value of satellite cloud photographs—particularly those of cloud forms along fronts—in improving forecasts. Above: conventional analysis of synoptic situation at 1500 GMT, showing cold front (A) in Bay of Biscay, based on extrapolation from 1200 GMT chart and a few ship observations at 1500 GMT. Right: TIROS nephanalysis for 1429 GMT received in time for preparation of 1800 GMT chart. This shows cloud which suggested that cold front A was in fact farther east than shown on conventional 1500 GMT chart. Later observations confirmed this, and the information was used to prepare a more accurate 1800 GMT forecast chart.

The Theory of Numerical Prediction

The work of Sutcliffe and Rossby was the prelude to a new approach to meteorological research in general, and weather forecasting in particular. Instead of simply watching the weather and establishing empirical relationships between various phenomena, meteorologists began to look at the circulation of the atmosphere as a whole and to think of it in terms of a problem of fluid mechanics and thermodynamics. The atmosphere is considered to be a fluid of varying density that is unevenly heated and subject to the spin and frictional effects of the underlying earth. These characteristics alone make the problem of prediction of a future state of the fluid a formidable one, but it is aggravated by the incompleteness of our description of the "initial" state of the fluid before calculation can begin. Despite these difficulties, for the past 20 years meteorologists have been wrestling with general hydrodynamic equations in attempts to apply them to the description and prediction of atmospheric behavior. Let us now take a look at the remarkable developments that have taken place during these 20 years and at the role of numerical weather prediction today.

The equations that are relevant to dynamic meteorology as a whole, as well as being basic to numerical forecasting, were formulated as general expressions of the principles of conservation of momentum, mass, and energy. Their relevance to meteorology was realized by a German named von Helmholtz as early as 1858 and was again stressed by V. Bjerknes early in this century. These *primitive* equations have been written in many ways but they always express the same relationship.

The *equation of motion* can be well summarized in a general dynamical equation relating the acceleration in any given direction to the component of force per unit mass acting in that direction. The *equation of continuity* states that any local increase or decrease in mass must be accounted for by import or export of mass in the region. The *thermodynamical equation* is derived from the First Law of Thermodynamics and states that any heat energy added to a system must be equal to the change in its internal energy plus the work done by it in expanding against pressure forces. The last relevant equation is the familiar *equation of state* based on Boyle's and Charles's laws for perfect gases, relating pressure to temperature and density.

These equations are a complete set in that there are four of them and there are four unknowns: temperature, pressure, density, and velocity. Given certain initial conditions, it should be possible with the use of these equations to calculate the values of the four parameters at a future time. This means that an initial distribution of pressure, temperature, and wind can be used to calculate a future distribution of these elements and once again provide the forecaster with a prebaratic chart. Numerical forecasting is simple in principle; in practice, however, many difficulties are still encountered.

There are two main reasons why numerical forecasting is not as simple as it would at first appear. First, the equations are very difficult to solve and, secondly, there was in the early days, and still is to some extent today, a deficiency of the right kind of data for this type of forecasting. The hydrodynamical equations are all expressed in terms of differentials—that is, the changes of an element (such as pressure) in space and time are described exactly and continuously in the language of calculus. Thus the differential expression relating pressure change to time over a period of one second, say, tells us the value of the rate of change at an infinite number of instances within that second (see diagram on page 117). The methods of calculus often allow us to work out solutions to differentials, but some equations that include differential expressions cannot be solved analytically. The hydrodynamical equations are of this type and new methods of solving them have to be used, as we shall see.

In the early stages of numerical prediction the second great stumbling block was the lack of upper-air data. We have seen in Chapter 2 how relatively sparse today's upper-air observations are; before World War II the position was far worse. The widespread use of the radiosonde has gone some way toward overcoming this obstacle, but we shall see in Chapter 6 that there are plans to increase further the data from these sources.

Despite these great difficulties, the potentialities of a purely dynamic approach to forecasting were realized late in the 19th century by the Norwegian V. Bjerknes. By the 1920s, the world had seen a heroic attempt by the Englishman L. F. Richardson to put the theory into practice. Recently Richardson's work has been much praised and many summaries of his glorious failure have been made. However, no treatment of numerical weather prediction would be complete without due recognition of Richardson's work, and the author makes no apology for describing again his major contribution.

Richardson appreciated the difficulties of solving analytically the hydrodynamical equations and made good use of a method whereby they could be solved by purely numerical procedure. In fact, he provided the basic routine of numerical prediction as used today. Richardson developed the *finite difference* method of solution, whereby a continuous variable (such as pressure distribution) is represented by its values at a *finite* number of discrete and closely spaced points and the changes in the variable are approximated by the *difference* between its values at these points. In practice this means the application of a grid to a field of, for instance, pressure or contours and using this grid to get approximations of the differentials that occur in the hydrodynamical equations—that is, the differential coefficients are replaced by finite differences.

Using this approximation of change of variable in *space*, we can calculate the initial rate of change in *time* of each variable from the hydrodynamical equations. Thus, we know the initial values of the variable (the analyzed pressure field, for example) and we know the initial rate of change; this means we can extrapolate the value of the variable over a very short time interval at each point in the grid. The final step is to use this calculated distribution as a new set of initial data and repeat the process. By this means, it is theoretically possible to build up a forecast over a period of time from a series of forecasts for much shorter intervals of time, usually an hour. Richardson used this method (his grid is illustrated on page 118) but found that his results were quite unrealistic. In fact he predicted a pressure change over Germany of 145 mb. in six hours. The reasons for his failure are now understood: it was mainly due to poor and inadequate data. But Richardson's approach provided the blueprint for the developments in the 1940s in the United States.

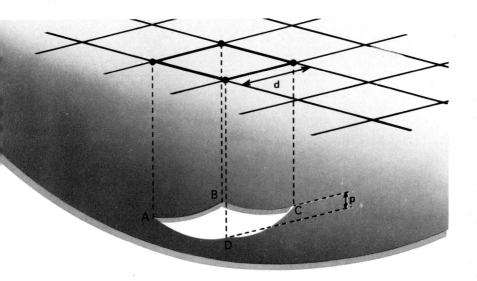

Numerical forecasting depends upon the finite difference method of solving the four fundamental equations described on page 114. A continuous variable, such as the blue surface, must be represented by its values at discrete, closely spaced points, such as A, B, C, D. The shape of the surface must be described in terms of the differences (p) between the values at these points, which are small but finite distances (d) apart, instead of by the more accurate, but less soluble, methods of calculus. As shown, a grid is superimposed onto the surface so that the finite distances are all equal and only the value of the meteorological element varies.

Inspired by Richardson's methodology, the increase in data brought about by the necessities of war, and the building of computers, several workers in the United States started a concentrated attack on the problem of numerical prediction in the late 1940s. The reader may feel that the finite difference method would solve all the problems the workers might encounter, but in fact it is only a beginning. The equations considered early in this section are of the most general form and this means that their solutions, however they are calculated, describe many types of wave motion in the atmosphere, some of them not meteorologically significant. Most small waves, such as sound waves, are not important in a meteorological context. On the other hand, waves of the Rossby dimensions, which are also solutions to the hydrodynamical equations, are vital cogs in the atmospheric machine and appear to be basic to the initiation and movement of weather-bearing systems. It is obviously desirable to exclude solutions of the hydrodynamical equations that correspond to small waves, at the same time retaining the solutions corresponding to the Rossby waves. This is known as the *filtering problem* and was tackled by J. G. Charney in 1948. By 1950 a mathematical model of the atmosphere that used the modified, or filtered, hydrodynamical equations gave the first numerical forecast from real initial conditions. This first attempt at a 24-hour forecast was undertaken in the US on the ENIAC computer under the direction of J. von Neuman, Charney, and R. Fjørtof at Aberdeen, Maryland; it took 24 hours of machine time. Since that rather shaky start, much progress has been made; in 1955 the Joint Numerical Weather Prediction Unit in the United States started to issue forecasts based on charts produced by numerical methods. Other countries were not as confident of their own methods in the mid-fifties; for example, it was not until November 1965 that the British Meteorological Office issued its first forecast based on numerical methods.

In all numerical weather-prediction units, mathematical models of the atmosphere are used. The earliest ones were so crude as to bear little resemblance to the real atmosphere, but later models are more realistic. The models fall into two main types: the *barotropic* and the *baroclinic* (see pages 120 and 121).

The barotropic model attempts to simulate the behavior of the whole atmosphere by analyzing motion at one level only. In

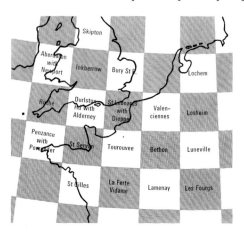

First attempt at a numerical forecast was made by Englishman L. F. Richardson, who, in 1910, attempted a six-hour forecast for an area in Germany. A section of his actual grid is shown here: pressure was observed at center of each blue checker, velocity at center of each white checker.

J. von Neuman and the ENIAC digital computer used to produce one of the earliest computerized numerical forecasts in 1952. Several 12-hour predictions were made covering the continental United States, each involving some 800,000 multiplications and requiring about one hour of continuous computing time. Computers currently used by ESSA take one hour and 23 minutes from input to production of 24-hour forecast maps, and require about 288 million additions and 144 million multiplications.

doing so, no consideration is given to the very real phenomena of vertical motion, frictional effects of the earth's surface, and *nonadiabatic* temperature changes (that is, those involving the addition and subtraction of heat) in the atmosphere. These omissions are not as drastic as they appear at first sight, if we consider motion at the 500-mb. level (about 5500 m.). First of all let us look at the problem of vertical motion. This is essentially a result of the configuration of divergence and convergence throughout the depth of the troposphere. The phenomenon of convergence underlying divergence, or vice versa, implies a level of nondivergence, which, as we noted earlier in considering Rossby's work, is usually taken to be at the 500-mb. level. So,

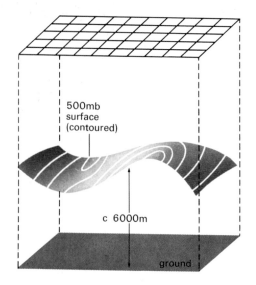

500mb surface (contoured)

c 6000m

ground

The simplest model used for making numerical forecasts is the barotropic or one-level one shown here. Values are calculated for each intersection in the superimposed grid. Limitation of the model in working out essentially three-dimensional developments is that results only describe motion for one surface (here the 500-mb. surface), that is, motion in two dimensions only. There is no consideration of vertical motion.

if any *one* level *has* to be taken as representative of large-scale atmospheric flow, as in the case of the barotropic model, the 500-mb. surface fills the bill. Although the model does not include frictional effects, this was not considered too great a drawback in the early stages of numerical prediction because these effects tend to be restricted to the lowest layers of the atmosphere anyway. The assumption that temperature changes are adiabatic has been shown by experience in synoptic analysis to be eminently reasonable—large-scale systems lasting for a few days *do* behave as if their thermal processes are adiabatic. Within this framework of qualifying factors, the solution of the equations uses the assumption that the winds in the atmospheric circulation are geostrophic or very nearly so. This is known as the *geostrophic approximation* and when it is applied selectively to some of the equations it acts as a filter that eliminates the irrelevant small-wave solutions.

We can summarize, then, by saying that the barotropic model allows us to calculate the future contour distribution of the 500-mb. surface. The reader will note that such a prediction is by no means a *weather* forecast in the strict sense, but it is the numerical equivalent of the prontour charts produced by the synoptic method.

Despite its crudity the barotropic model produced good results and encouraged workers to continue research into

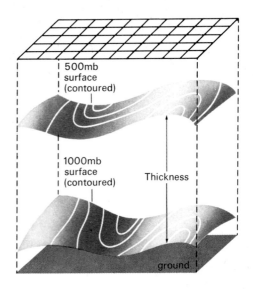

In the two-level baroclinic model shown here, values are calculated for intersections on the same grid superimposed on two pressure levels, here the 500- and 1000-mb. surfaces. This makes it possible to work out thickness and vertical velocities in between these two surfaces, with a consequent improvement in forecast accuracy. Operational forecasts may use up to five levels, but experiments on 10-level models have been carried out.

500mb surface (contoured)

1000mb surface (contoured)

Thickness

ground

numerical methods. The greatest deficiency of this model is its inability to predict *cyclogenesis* (the development of cyclonic circulation), and this led to the development of the *baroclinic* model, used to predict the flow at several levels in the atmosphere. The primary differences between the barotropic and the baroclinic model are that in the latter the winds vary from one level to another and the temperature distribution is not dependent solely on the pressure distribution. The baroclinic model is therefore a more accurate representation of the atmosphere than the barotropic one.

The early baroclinic models considered only two levels and retained the geostrophic approximation as a filter (see diagram on this page). They succeeded in predicting cyclogenesis but not at the right times and right places, or at the correct rate. Also, the prediction of the mid-tropospheric flow patterns (i.e. at 500 mb.) were not significantly better than those of the barotropic model. Such results were disappointing but there were redeeming features. The solutions of the equations were in terms of one parameter only—height of pressure surfaces—and this allowed the calculation of other parameters, such as vertical velocities. This was a great step forward, as the predicted patterns of vertical motion corresponded very well with the observed patterns of precipitation and cloud cover.

Later developments in the baroclinic model followed two

main avenues. The number of levels for which the predictions were made was increased—at first to three or six, until today even ten-level models are used experimentally. This increase in the number of levels obviously increases the resolution of the calculations and leads to a more accurate description of flows. The second development is a continuing reappraisal of the filtering problem. Both the barotropic and the baroclinic models considered up to now employed the geostrophic approximation as a filtering device. It proved to be so efficient at excluding small-wave solutions that mathematicians began to wonder whether it was too efficient and whether it was possible to use a less restrictive approximation that would still do the job. This is an important point because in reality many winds do *not* take on geostrophic values. It appears that the geostrophic models (i.e. models with the geostrophic approximation) considered up to this point reproduce the general features of the atmospheric circulation but fall down on detail. The refining of the filter mechanism is proving a difficult task, but the day is fast approaching when the equations in their general unmodified form (the *primitive* equations as outlined earlier in this section) will be used. This return to square one is the result of a breakthrough in the late 1950s by workers in Norway, the United States, and Germany, who successfully integrated a multilevel atmospheric model with the primitive equations, thus giving us the "partly filtered nongeostrophic model." This is characterized by the direct use of the equations of motion as prognostic equations, the omission of the geostrophic approximation, the inclusion of so-called "noise components," and the necessity to specify initially two horizontal wind components and the geopotential. The main attraction of using the primitive equations is that for a baroclinic model, the equations are simpler and the computer programming is easier. This form of numerical prediction is still in the development stage and at present we must still rely on the multilevel baroclinic model for one- to two-day forecasts and the barotropic model for three- to four-day forecasts.

The above is a very brief review of the general methodology and models used in numerical prediction. But these complex methods of calculation are useless without two things— adequate data in the right form describing the initial state of the atmosphere, and some means of completing the calculations in time for the results to be of practical use in forecasting. The first requirement, as we saw in Chapter 3, is being taken care of; highspeed electronic computers provide the answer to the second. Richardson suggested that to keep ahead of the weather by means of numerical forecasting would need 64,000 trained human computers working night and day. Today, electronic digital computers are fast enough to produce 24-hour forecasts by numerical methods. The combination of computers and a sufficient amount of upper-air and surface data has already allowed the development of objective analysis of meteorological fields. In Chapter 3 we noted that surface and upper-air chart analysis has, throughout the history of the subject, been done by hand. We also noted how this method was susceptible to subjective judgment. In objective analysis the aim is to receive information, check it, store it, plot it, and draw isopleths on charts without the intervention of subjective human interpretation. It is of course in the drawing of isopleths by an analyst that the subjective element really comes to the fore. By devising a technique for objective analysis we therefore kill two birds with one stone: the analysis itself is probably more accurate than could be achieved by conventional procedure; and it provides the basis for the numerical forecast.

The Practice of Numerical Prediction

How can we achieve an objective analysis geared to the finite-difference method of prediction? First, it is necessary to have a grid over the area to be considered. The density of the grid varies with the size of the area covered and with the particular model being used. The one used by the United States Weather Bureau's National Meteorological Center for its North American forecasts is shown on page 124. It will be seen that the grid covers a far larger area than the forecast area. This is to minimize the errors that arise from the grid boundary that provides a horizontal limit to the atmospheric simulation— a limit that does not of course exist in reality.

1000 km

The first requirement for a numerical forecast is a suitable grid. The one shown here is used by the United States Weather Bureau's National Meteorological Center for its North American forecasts. Grid overlaps forecast area to avoid errors resulting from imposing an essentially artificial horizontal limit to atmospheric phenomena.

Opposite: this United States Weather Bureau data plotter produces 24-hour upper-air pressure and wind predictions for the Northern Hemisphere by numerical methods. The map shown here was drawn in three minutes by attaching a small light to the plotting arm.

Once the grid has been decided upon, values of pressure, temperature, or any other element used in the analysis are assigned to the intersections on the grid by statistical manipulation of the data from the surface and upper-air networks. It is of course possible to do this with the relevant data every time an analysis is made, but current procedure allows the use of a short cut. The raw data are fed into a computer that has been instructed how to recognize and store data relevant to the desired analysis to be made. Then the most recent forecast of the present state is fed into the machine, again in terms of numbers on a grid. The computer then has all the current observations and an expectation based on past history. Forecast observations are given much less weight than the real ones. Around any grid intersection is set up the linear function that best fits the observations in the vicinity of the point, and a field value is then obtained for that intersection. This is done for all the points on the grid. The result is then tested to see whether the interpolated values at observing stations differ greatly from the actual observed values. If the difference is great, the whole procedure is repeated until interpolated and observed values agree. Obviously the weight given to the previous forecast values in the initial stages varies with the availability of observed values. In the land areas of the United States and Europe the previous forecast values play a minor role, but over the oceans they become very important.

The technique of this type of analysis is quite complicated, but fortunately programs and machines exist to carry through the operation. Difficulties do arise however on a more mundane level—that of communication of the data. There are two major shortcomings in the present communications structure from the point of view of numerical weather prediction. First, data for a hemisphere are not available for six hours, mainly because the transmitting channels are overloaded. This problem is aggravated by factors such as messages having a low information content and occasionally triplicating the same information. Secondly, the content and form of the data are not at present very well suited to numerical weather analysis. Internationally recognized code forms are not rigidly adhered to and there are no checks on the internal consistency of a single message. Apart from these two specific problems there is the more general one of considerable redundancy in the data from the real atmosphere as far as its vertical structure is concerned. It is considered that if we have data for five levels above a given point on the earth's surface, taken from the bottom 90 per cent of the mass of the atmosphere, we can interpolate to obtain values for intermediate levels with sufficient accuracy for almost any practical purpose. In fact, few meteorological services use five-level models for prediction of large-scale circulation.

At present about 25 services are engaged in routine and experimental work in numerical methods of data extraction, analysis, and prediction. With the exception of China, Israel, Japan, and South Africa, all the services are in the USSR, the United States, Europe, or the British Commonwealth. In Sweden the air force has a project separate from that of the national meteorological service, and in the United States both the air force and the navy produce routine analysis and predictions independently of the Weather Bureau. Of the 25 services involved in numerical work only the following nine undertake data extraction, analysis, and prediction on a routine basis: Canada, Japan, Norway, Swedish Air Force, Sweden, United Kingdom, United States Air Force, United States Navy, and United States Weather Bureau.

Most of the services use barotropic models but the British Meteorological Office and most of the United States services employ three-level baroclinic models. The United States Weather Bureau's National Meteorological Center started using this model in 1962, when meteorologists were satisfied that it had forecast correctly at least some of the conversions of potential to kinetic energy in the atmosphere and that it had less overall error than the barotropic model. The vertical structure of the atmosphere is represented in this model by data at three levels: 850 mb. (about 1500 m. above sea level); 500 mb. (about 5500 m.); and 200 mb. (about 13,000 m.). The grid is shown on page 124. The British model uses the 1000-mb., 500-mb. (or 600-mb.) and 200-mb. levels, and has a grid of 24×20

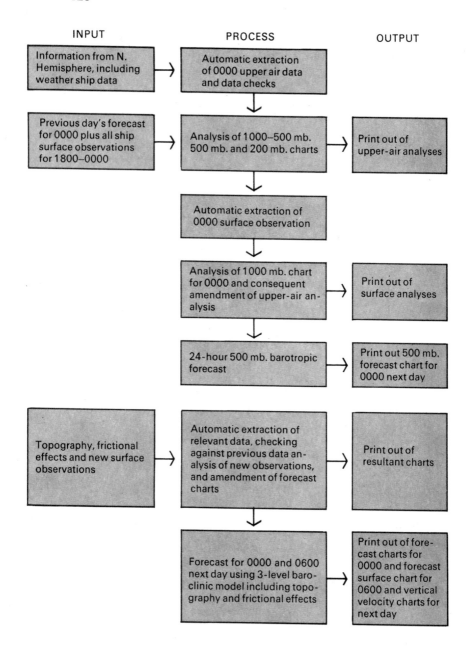

INPUT   PROCESS   OUTPUT

Information from N. Hemisphere, including weather ship data → Automatic extraction of 0000 upper air data and data checks

Previous day's forecast for 0000 plus all ship surface observations for 1800–0000 → Analysis of 1000–500 mb. 500 mb. and 200 mb. charts → Print out of upper-air analyses

Automatic extraction of 0000 surface observation

Analysis of 1000 mb. chart for 0000 and consequent amendment of upper-air analysis → Print out of surface analyses

24-hour 500 mb. barotropic forecast → Print out 500 mb. forecast chart for 0000 next day

Topography, frictional effects and new surface observations → Automatic extraction of relevant data, checking against previous data analysis of new observations, and amendment of forecast charts → Print out of resultant charts

Forecast for 0000 and 0600 next day using 3-level baroclinic model including topography and frictional effects → Print out of forecast charts for 0000 and forecast surface chart for 0600 and vertical velocity charts for next day points extending from Hudson Bay to Russia with a mesh size of about 300 km. Both models include an approximation of the effects of surface friction but neither takes account of the liberation of latent heat.

The actual operation of a typical numerical forecast is illustrated opposite. We can see that the output consists of forecast charts of surface pressure, 500-mb. contours and vertical velocities for the 1000–600-mb. layer. The United States produces charts of the heights of 300-mb., 500-mb., and 850-mb. surfaces and the vertical air speed at the 600-mb. surface.

The accuracy of the charts varies with the type of model used for their calculation. The examples on page 131 illustrate the capabilities of different models.

The maps A, B, and C show the contours of the 500-mb. surface associated with the development of a storm over New England. A deep depression at the 500-mb. level developed over a period of 36 hours from the time of map A. Map D shows the result of a forecast of this development using the barotropic model, and we see that it completely failed to show the actual development. The forecast from a three-level baroclinic model is shown in map E, and this indicates the general pattern but fails to show the extent of the development. Map F, constructed from an experimental four-level primitive equation model, illustrates a forecast that, while not at all perfect, is substantially better than the others.

Finally, it is important to stress that numerical methods do not, on a routine basis, predict the actual weather. What they do predict by objective methods are the future circulations at the surface and in the upper air; it still remains for the forecaster to put in the actual weather, in terms of cloud cover, precipitation, and the like. The distribution of vertical velocities as given by the computer is helpful in this operation, and research is continuing into the possibility of computing some

Opposite: simplified flow-chart shows typical procedure for numerical forecasting. The times given are not necessarily accurate but are included to give some idea of the sequence of events.

parts of the synoptic fine structure. At the other end of the scale from synoptic fine structure lie the hemispherical circulations, which are the fundamental mechanisms behind the weather. In fact they form the main cogs of the general circulation of the atmosphere and, as such, have been subject to numerical analysis in attempts to unravel the main driving forces in the atmosphere. These analyses of large-scale motions are particularly relevant to long-range forecasting—a subject to which we now turn.

Long-Range Forecasting

Accurate long-range forecasts would have a tremendously beneficial effect on mankind. Although most meteorologists are very aware of the potential benefits, few are actually involved in research into and routine use of long-range prediction in most national meteorological services. Indeed, the methods employed are often the brainchild of an individual research worker who is convinced that his method is superior to any other, and the whole field of long-range prediction is so full of uncertainties that few of his colleagues would dare to challenge his insight into the long-term workings of the atmosphere. Yet it is a field in which there are so many possibilities open for the operation of causal factors that it is almost true that any worker could say "Your guess (or method) is as good as mine."

There is no strict definition of the period covered by a long-range forecast. In fact, a review of the literature suggests that anything longer than the two to three days normally covered by the short-range forecast would qualify as long-range. One issued specifically for a five-day period is on the other hand considered by most authorities to be of an "extended" rather than "long-range" type. In 1962 about 15 countries issued forecasts for one- to two-week periods in purely qualitative statements. Forecasts for one month ahead were issued by the following countries: West Germany, France, East Germany, Japan, Turkey, USSR, UK, and USA. Of these only USA, USSR, France, West Germany, and East Germany gave quantitative forecasts. The other services produced only qualitative descriptions in general terms of the weather to be

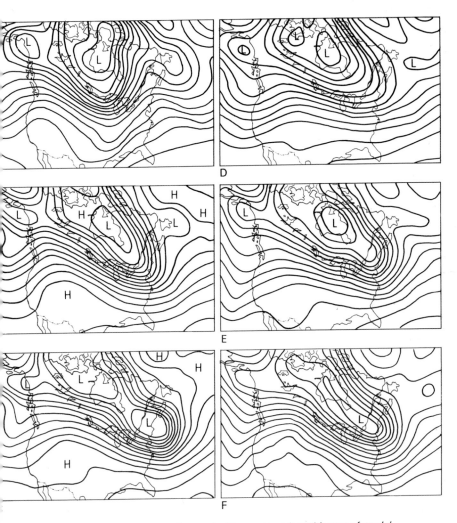

Charts showing how accuracy of numerical forecasts varies with type of model used. Charts A, B, and C show actual contours of the 500-mb. surface at times t, t + 24 hours, and t + 36 hours respectively; development of a storm over New England is clearly shown. Other charts are a 36-hour barotropic forecast made at t (D); a 36-hour forecast from an operational three-level baroclinic model (E); and a 36-hour forecast from a four-level primitive-equation model (F). The significance of these charts is discussed in the text.

expected in their areas. Seasonal forecasts, by far the most ambitious type of long-range prediction, are of necessity rather vague statements about anomalies of temperature and precipitation for a two- to three-month period over a large area. Most research into seasonal prediction is naturally carried out in countries whose economies are heavily dependent on seasonal changes in weather. The most familiar example is that of forecasting the beginning and end of the monsoon by the Indian, Pakistani, and Indonesian meteorological services. This will be dealt with in more detail later in this chapter. In mid-latitudes, West Germany and the United States both issue seasonal forecasts, and experiments were undertaken by East Germany and Turkey in 1958.

The problem of long-range weather prediction is closely allied to the central problem of meteorology—the general circulation of the atmosphere. If this were fully understood, and a theory explaining its behavior available, there would be no difficulty about long-range prediction and very little to delay substantial progress in conscious weather modification. In fact, of course, we know all too little about the general circulation, even at the descriptive stage. This is made very clear to us when we learn that full investigations into the hot summer of 1959 and the very severe winter of 1962–63 in the British Isles have not revealed any definite causal factors. To quote one of the investigators: "Frankly we do not understand these things yet." Such failures would appear to make any attempt at long-term prognosis an impertinence. But if scientists were daunted by past failures there would be little advance in our knowledge and understanding.

The reasons for the failure to make forecasting more long-term are not hard to establish. Workers experienced in the ways of the atmospheric circulation are familiar with the spatial and temporal dimensions of the systems that give us most of our weather. With the use of the methods outlined earlier in this chapter it is possible to forecast the development and movement of such systems over their lifetime of a few days. This is completely different from attempting to forecast the *existence* and *whereabouts* of such systems; and this is the essence of the long-range forecast problem. Consequently, to quote Sutcliffe: "there is . . . a natural limitation to the period of detailed forecasts, a kind of time-barrier through which it is proving extraordinarily difficult to penetrate however much we may advance in scientific understanding. . . ." In view of the difficulty of the problem there is little wonder that a former Director-General of the British Meteorological Office, Sir Graham Sutton, wrote: "I should regard the long-range forecasting problem as solved for most practical purposes if I knew of any method which could produce a statement like the following:

'. . . In the south east of England the coming month will begin with generally cyclonic weather, with temperatures 2° to 4° below average, rainfall about 25 per cent above average and fresh to strong winds. After about 10 days there will be a change to settled anticyclonic weather, with temperatures a little above average, little or no rain, few clouds, and generally light winds. This weather is expected to continue at least until the end of the period. . . .'

provided that it was verified on 80 to 90 per cent of occasions."

In practice the British Meteorological Office issues monthly forecasts typified by the following one for July 1967:

"Although the weather is likely to become unsettled in most areas within a few days, several more anticyclonic spells are expected later, especially in the south. However, towards the end of the month, unsettled weather will probably become more frequent again in most districts.

"Rainfall for July is likely to be below the seasonal average in northeastern, eastern, southeastern England and the Midlands, and not far from the average over Scotland, Northern Ireland, Wales, and western areas of England. In many parts of England and Wales thunderstorms, though not more frequent than usual, will probably contribute much of the month's rainfall.

"The mean monthly temperature is expected to be above the seasonal average in all parts of Britain and Northern Ireland except for north Scotland where near-average temperatures are expected."

The main difference between these two "forecasts" is in the figures that Sutton gives. Apart from this there is little to choose between them. Yet most long-range forecasters hope to be able to improve on their present performance: a performance that is a result of the application of methods to be outlined below. As already suggested, a great variety of long-range forecasting techniques have been tried and tested. However, it is possible to recognize three categories into one or more of which most techniques fall. They are the statistical, the physical, and the synoptic categories. Purely statistical techniques rest on simple correlations between weather elements by regression formulas. The physical category covers a multitude of techniques ranging from the dynamic approach to vorticity conservation (as in the case of short-range numerical prediction), through thermal considerations of the changing heat sources and sinks on the earth's surface, to the possible responses of the atmosphere to solar variability. Synoptic techniques form two main subcategories: the extrapolation of synoptic mean charts, a method favored by the Extended Forecast Section of the United States Weather Bureau; and the use of analogues, the method favored by the British Meteorological Office.

Statistical Methods

Superficially perhaps the most ambitious long-range forecast is one that attempts to predict the weather for a whole season. However, if we remember that in certain parts of the world some seasons have reasonably well-defined limits and characteristics, seasonal forecasting becomes a less daunting problem. The best example is probably the monsoon rain climate of the Indian subcontinent. Ever since the first official forecast of the coming monsoon, issued in June 1886, the Indian meteorological service has been preparing forecasts of the coming rains and is continuing research into the statistical methods used. The real foundation for these studies was laid by Sir Gilbert Walker when he was head of the Indian meteorological service between 1904 and 1924. He introduced objective methods into monsoon forecasting, particularly the correlation approach for testing the validity of relationships between the rainfall to be forecast and various factors. Factors found statistically significant were taken up for further analysis before they were included in a linear regression equation. In all, 30 factors for evolving regression formulas for monsoon forecasting were selected. Four of these factors were: South American pressure; snow accumulation in the Himalayas; Zanzibar rainfall; and Ceylon rainfall. The reader will notice how remote from the Indian monsoon some of these factors are. The Indians stress that this method of long-range forecasting is purely statistical and consequently there are many dangers possible in the careless manipulations of figures. The lack of physical understanding is well illustrated by the fact that there is a high correlation between the rainfall of peninsular and northwest India and the South American pressure factor. This has been a dominant factor in the operational monsoon forecast formulas for several decades and yet there is no explanation for the relationship.

The following is a typical forecast prepared by the use of statistical methods:

"Memorandum regarding the probable amount of monsoon rainfall in 1964 [issued June 11, 1964].

"For the peninsula: the statistical analysis indicates that there is a four to one chance that the monsoon rainfall in the peninsula during June to September 1964 will be above 112 per cent of the normal rainfall. For northwest India [the monsoon rainfall] will be above 117 per cent of the normal rainfall."

Such a forecast appears to be quite definite in its quantitative statement but really the figures are only intended to give a rough idea of whether there will be more or less rain than usual. The Indian meteorological service is "fully aware of the limitations of the correlation approach and the need for a physical understanding and basis in the selection of factors." However, it is still persevering with this method.

Physical Methods

In attempts to take into account the necessary "physical understanding," some national meteorological centers have made efforts to apply the numerical technique to long-range forecasting. In view of the recent successes of numerical methods in short-range forecasts, it would seem obvious simply to extend the time interval over which the computations are made. There are two reasons why this is not done: first, the natural time limit for the evolution of weather systems mentioned on page 132; and, secondly, the errors in the calculations, which increase with time and markedly reduce the quality of the predicted chart. Despite these two difficulties, some headway has been made in the application of numerical methods to long-range prediction, mainly by workers in the United States and the USSR.

With the use of the barotropic model and data from the whole of the northern hemisphere, it is possible to achieve some success with a forecast for three days ahead. If numerical methods are combined with the conventional synoptic methods (as they are in the United States) there is a definite improvement in a five-day forecast. Such "extended" forecasts have been prepared in the United States since 1958. But for really long-range forecasts by numerical methods we must turn to the USSR. In the period 1952–58 the World Meteorological Center in Moscow prepared experimental forecasts of winds and temperature anomalies for large areas of the Soviet Union for periods of 40 to 70 days. A much modified barotropic model was used for the wind forecast, and a modified form of the thermodynamic equation was used for the temperature prediction. These forecasts have been continued and supplemented since 1961 by operational forecasts of the mean monthly vertical velocities over the Northern Hemisphere for 40 days in advance. Although the present methods of hydrodynamical long-range forecasting require even greater simplification of the general equations than do those for short-range forecasting, they represent an approach that, according to E. N. Blinova of the Hydrometeorological Service of the USSR, "has the aim of taking into account not only weather-forming factors, but also climate-forming factors." As such, they are tackling the most fundamental problem of meteorology.

Synoptic Methods

Midway between the statistical and the physical approach, and less ambitious than either from the point of view of time covered by the forecast, is the synoptic method of long-range

Monsoon clouds gather over the Indian countryside. Statistical methods used by the Indian meteorological service for monsoon forecasting are based upon analyses of as many as 30 factors, some of them as remote as South American pressure, snow accumulation in the Himalayas, Zanzibar rainfall, and Ceylon rainfall.

prediction. Variations on this basic technique have found favor in the meteorological services of the United States and the United Kingdom. In the United States the real attack on the long-range problem began as early as 1935, as a joint undertaking by the Weather Bureau, the Bureau of Agricultural Economics, and the Department of Meteorology of the Massachusetts Institute of Technology. From that time to the present day, development has been under the general guidance of J. Namias, and the greater part of the technique now in use is due to work by or under the immediate direction of Namias. In the United Kingdom, long-range forecasting, in common with all forecast development, was under the general supervision of R. C. Sutcliffe throughout the 1950s. It has tended not to have major priority in the United Kingdom, probably through lack of funds for a project that, at first sight, looks rather speculative.

In the United States the Extended Forecast Branch is in the same building as the Joint Numerical Weather Prediction Unit. This means that the Extended Forecast Branch can receive a large proportion of its working material from the JNWPU in a form suitable for a computer. This is particularly useful for data processing. The presence of the main library of the Weather Bureau is an added advantage.

The main work of the Extended Forecast Branch is the preparation of forecasts of the mean conditions for periods of

5 days and 30 days ahead. This is done by estimating future changes from a series of Northern Hemisphere charts of the observed height of the 700-mb. surface averaged over the same period. Once the forecast chart has been produced, the actual weather conditions, usually in terms of temperature and rainfall, are obtained. Here again we see the essence of the synoptic method. The five-day forecasts are derived from an extrapolation of the changes on a series of overlapping five-day mean charts. The extrapolation is helped by short-range numerical forecasts and by the assumption that five-day mean upper-air features will be advected by barotropic processes. The final forecast includes a prediction of the 700-mb. contour field for the Northern Hemisphere for the five-day period, a similar forecast of the mean pressure field at sea level and the distribution of temperature and rainfall anomalies over the United States. The 30-day forecasts tend to be the preserve of Namias himself, and their preparation is at the stage that short-term synoptic forecasting was at before the war, in that the experience of the forecaster plays a large part in deciding the accuracy of the prediction. In the forecasting procedure many factors are taken into account: climatic norms and the relationships of mean circulation patterns to weather and storm tracks provide the essential empirical background; the nature of the physical characteristics and evolution of 30-day mean circulations are of course important; and kinematic and dynamic analyses allow the actual extrapolation to be made. Upon the completion of the prognostic mean 700-mb. contour chart, the expected anomalies of temperature and rainfall at the surface must be derived.

The other important synoptic technique for long-range prediction is the one employed by the British Meteorological Office. Based upon the analogue approach, it is perhaps the least "scientific" in that there is no attempt at theoretical treatment or even extrapolation based on some insight into past trends. The method used is to search through all previous years' records (some 80 years are available) to find a situation that had a history as similar as possible to the present one, and to assume that development of the present one will follow closely development of the analogue. The features used in the comparison are monthly mean patterns of 1000–500 mb. thicknesses, mean surface pressure patterns, and sequences of synoptic weather situations. An example of such a forecast was given on page 133. Although much research went into long-range forecasting, it was not until December 1963 that the first monthly forecast was published by the British Meteorological Office. Since then an accuracy test, carried out over a period of 33 months, showed that moderate agreement between forecast and actual conditions of temperature and rainfall was obtained on 73 per cent of the occasions. Such a figure hides the many inaccuracies evident in a more detailed analysis; for instance, average rainfall being forecast 49 per cent of the time occurring on only 35 per cent of occasions.

Many books and thousands of papers have been written on the subject of forecasting in general. But both long-range and numerical short-range forecasting bring us up against the same central problem—the general circulation. Because some meteorologists perhaps feel that forecasting has progressed as far as it can, it is not surprising that they have turned hopefully to the possibilities of weather modification—the subject of the next chapter.

5 Modification

Much has been written in the past 20 years on the possibilities of weather modification and many of the early writers were a little too optimistic about what could be done. The fact that even now we can only hope to forecast the weather in any detail up to three days ahead should serve as a warning that our understanding of the atmospheric circulations is still so limited as to make conscious, controlled modification of the weather over any area, large or small, very much a thing of the future. It is not, however, unreasonable for the physical scientists who study the atmosphere to hope that one day they will have some control over what goes on in their outdoor laboratory. There has, after all, already been unconscious modification of certain atmospheric characteristics on quite a large scale. For instance, the increase of carbon dioxide in the Northern Hemisphere atmosphere from 290 parts per million prior to 1900 to 330 parts per million today, and the consequent slight increase in overall temperature, are due largely to the burning of fossil

Since World War II cloud seeding to make rain has become scientifically respectable and reasonably reliable. Top: cumulus cloud over New South Wales, with top at about 6000 m. and −12°C, base at 2000 m., +10°C. Below: same cloud 40 minutes after seeding with 30 gm. of silver iodide, released from an aircraft in the form of smoke. Rain caused by seeding is clearly visible.

fuels over this period. Similarly the remarkable growth of urban areas in the present century has led to an aggravation of the air pollution and smog problem with, as we saw in Chapter 1, serious consequences. These are probably the most important examples of man's unconscious influence upon the atmospheric processes because they have both immediate and, potentially, long-term effects on man's well-being. A far more spectacular means of modifying weather is by nuclear explosion —short-lived and comparatively local, but capable of releasing, in one instant, as much energy as is converted in the course of one thunderstorm (see diagram on page 163).

The possibility of altering atmospheric characteristics has proved very tempting to many meteorologists, particularly in the United States. The discoveries of Langmuir, Schaefer, and Vonnegut in the late 1940s (to be outlined later) released a spate of literature on the possibilities of modifying clouds. This tampering with clouds was important in two respects. First, it was concerned with meteorological phenomena that could be studied in the laboratory with familiar experimental techniques of classical physics. At last, it seemed, a feature of the atmosphere had been found that was subject to the laws of exact science and must therefore be capable of controlled experimentation. Secondly, individual clouds, or even small cloud agglomerations, are part of the synoptic fine structure and as such have little part to play in the fundamental energy exchanges and fluxes that drive the atmospheric circulation. The exploitation of the first point and the lack of appreciation of the second, meant that nearly all attempts at weather modification between 1946 and 1960 tended to be hopeful shots in the dark rather than sober investigations.

In the period 1946 to the early 1960s weather modification was synonymous with cloud seeding, in the broadest sense. Because of this, modification has also been very closely linked with basic research into cloud physics, particularly the microphysics of precipitation particle formation, and its history has been justifiably divided into four periods. The first period (1911–45) is strictly pre-modification, but, because it gave rise to basic theories of precipitation, it forms a necessary back-

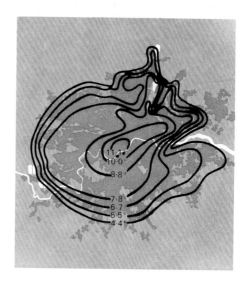

Man's unconscious modification of weather and climate is a phenomenon familiar to meteorologists. Temperatures over built-up areas, for example, are usually higher than surrounding country, especially at night. Map shows minimum-temperature isotherms in London on May 14, 1959, when a deep anticyclone over Europe allowed formation of an intense heat island over the city.

cloth. The second period (1946–7) is perhaps the critical one in that it saw the discovery of effective ice-nucleating agents. The third period (1947–54) saw the early exploratory experiments into cloud modification, and the fourth period (1955 to the present) is one of more fundamental tests and even of some commercial efforts. To some extent the tests are of the type that one feels should have been proposed after the discoveries in 1947. But it is easy to be wise after the event.

Although cloud seeding forms a large part of weather modification, there are many other interesting aspects of the program. These, together with methods of influencing clouds and storm systems, are all considered in the report of a panel on Weather and Climate Modification, published in 1966 by the U.S. National Research Council, Washington, D.C., which forms the main source of material for much of this chapter.

Because clouds are the essence of "weather," in official books of weather observation as well as to the layman, modification of clouds covers several aspects apart from the popular notion of rainmaking. It is true that early investigators had rainmaking as their main aim and it remains a major objective today, but redistribution of precipitation that would have fallen anyway is perhaps of equal importance. The other important aspects of cloud modification to be treated here are suppression of hail and lightning, fog clearance, and tornado and hurricane modification.

Rainmaking

For many centuries there have been individuals who claimed to be able to produce rain and, even today, some primitive tribes have faith in their witch doctor's ability to bring on a deluge. One of the most successful of the early rainmakers (though his success was perhaps mainly financial) was a certain Charles Hatfield who was born in Kansas in 1875. Hatfield "learned" his rainmaking in Los Angeles and in 1904 he "produced" 4.5 cm. of rain over the Sierra Madre in two days, thus winning a bet on his capabilities. During the next 20 years he conducted his rainmaking in a businesslike fashion mainly in the dry midwestern areas of North America. His actual apparatus consisted of large 8-m. towers with tanks of galvanized iron on top. The tanks were filled with iron trays containing chemicals believed to include copper sulfate. The trays were connected to the ground by copper wires that were said to carry electric charges. No indication was given of how this apparatus was supposed to produce rain, but Hatfield's luck seemed boundless. On nearly every occasion rain did occur, sometimes in copious quantities. In one experiment at Medicine Hat, Canada, the rainfall six days after erection of the structure totaled nearly 3 cm. and farmers began to ask Hatfield to turn it off.

This is only one example of the fascinating "methods" that have been employed in the past to stimulate rain. There is obviously no scientific basis to such efforts and indeed, it is only comparatively recently that rainmaking has taken on scientific respectability. Let us look at these recent developments in some detail.

The first exploratory steps in the precipitation initiation process were taken before World War II. By 1940, two main mechanisms for precipitation particle growth had been recognized. They were the ice-crystal (Bergeron) process and the coalescence process. It is perhaps worthwhile reminding ourselves of the main points of these mechanisms of natural growth of precipitation as they are vital to an appreciation of the techniques of cloud modification. The Bergeron process (diagramed opposite) operates in clouds that contain both ice crystals and droplets of supercooled water. Such a situation occurs

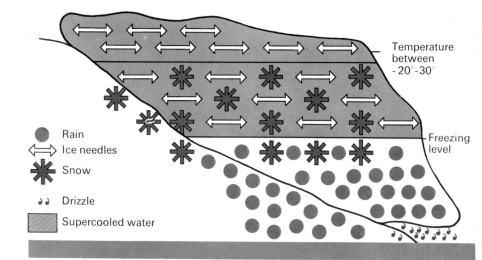

The Bergeron process suggests one way in which large drops of rain form in a cloud of very small drops. At top, cloud consists of ice needles (or crystals) and supercooled cloud drops. For reasons explained in text, the ice needles grow at the expense of the droplets, thus forming snowflakes that fall through the cloud, passing freezing level to fall out as rain. In addition, the enlarged ice needles or snowflakes splinter, explaining the formation of large numbers of large drops from relatively few ice crystals.

frequently in the atmosphere and is basic to the Bergeron mechanism. Because the saturation vapor pressure over ice is less than that over water, vapor that is only saturated with respect to water is supersaturated with respect to ice. Consequently, condensation occurs on the ice crystals at the expense of the supercooled water droplets. This condensation removes water vapor from the air, thus making it subsaturated relative to the water droplets; they begin to evaporate and thus replenish the water vapor supply of the crystals. In this way, the crystals grow at the expense of the water droplets and may reach a size that has a terminal velocity greater than that of the cloud updraft: consequently they fall out. The other mechanism for converting cloud droplets into precipitation drops is aimed at producing rainfall from clouds that do not contain ice crystals. It is reasonably certain that many droplets collide and coalesce thus producing particles large enough to fall out under their own weight. The problem of finding droplets of a sufficient size (radius at least 19 microns) for coalescence to occur has not really been solved, but it is suggested that giant condensation

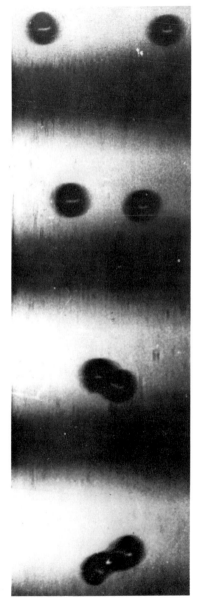

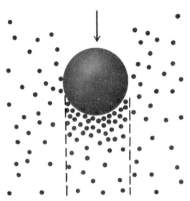

The coalescence theory explains the formation of rain in clouds that do not contain ice crystals: many droplets, it is suggested, collide and coalesce to form particles large enough to fall out under their own weight, collecting further droplets in their path as they fall (above), or pushing them aside with their cushion of air (below). Left: a rare sequence shows coalescence of falling water droplets (radius 120 microns) taking place under laboratory conditions.

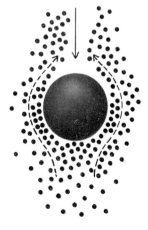

nuclei might favor rapid growth of the cloud droplets.

It was in the context of these two processes that the experiments of Schaefer, Langmuir, and Vonnegut were made. The apparent simplicity of the rain-producing mechanisms gave rise to high hopes of substantial modification and, despite the many setbacks suffered since 1947, the discoveries of that time still remain the basis of any practical cloud or weather modification. It is now time to outline the techniques employed.

The work of V. J. Schaefer, as well as that of I. Langmuir and B. Vonnegut, was undertaken in the General Electric Research Laboratory at Schenectady, New York. Schaefer was interested in the general cloud physics problem of the production and simulation of ice crystals. He found that at temperatures less than $-39°C$ spontaneous freezing of supercooled water took place. Using this result he showed that in a simple cold chamber, a cloud of supercooled liquid water could be converted to ice crystals by the introduction of an object at a temperature less than $-39°C$. Initially the object was a needle that had been dipped in liquid air, but Schaefer found that a tiny particle of solid carbon dioxide (Dry Ice) gave the same results. In the context of the Bergeron process, the implications of these results were truly enormous. Hopes were kept at a high level by one of the first experiments in the atmosphere in November 1946. A supercooled $(-18.5°C)$ altostratus cloud six kilometers long was "seeded" with 3 kg. of Dry Ice by flying through it in a small Fairchild monoplane at an altitude of 5000 m. Half the Dry Ice fragments were dispersed from a mechanical dispenser operating on the floor of the plane; the remainder were scattered by letting the slipstream suck the fragments from boxes held out of an open window. Such a simple large-scale replica of the laboratory experiment had the expected results of clearing a distinct lane in the cloud deck. Small wonder that meteorologists were optimistic.

At about the same time that Schaefer was assessing the possibilities of Dry Ice seeding, Vonnegut was working on a similar theme. In 1947 he found that silver iodide smoke had the property of causing snowflakes to form in a supercooled cloud. This is the same effect as that produced by Dry Ice, but the

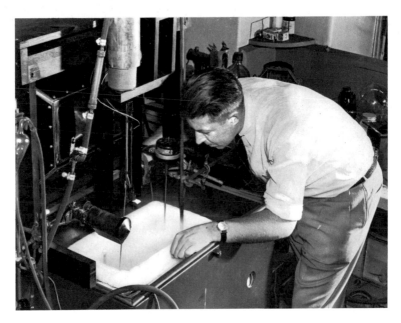

Dr. V. J. Schaefer studying supercooling with a domestic freezer at General Electric Research Laboratory. Hopes for cloud modification soared when, in 1946, he dropped a large piece of Dry Ice into the freezer: at once, air inside the freezer was full of ice crystals. Later the same year, Schaefer seeded a supercooled cloud with Dry Ice from an aircraft to produce an artificial snowstorm.

mechanism leading to it is completely different. Whereas Dry Ice merely cools the supercooled droplets to a temperature so low that they freeze spontaneously, silver iodide particles are good nuclei for ice formation because of the close resemblance of their crystal structure to that of ice. The particles do, in fact, act as freezing nuclei. In the initial experiment Vonnegut used a method of silver iodide smoke production that still provides the basis for the most efficient and economic way of seeding clouds. Two hundred grams of silver iodide and 100 gm. of ammonium iodide were mixed with 750 cm^3 of acetone and 250 cm^3 of water. This mixture was diluted to 10 times its volume with acetone, and smoke was produced by spraying the resultant solution into a hydrogen flame. The smoke particles varied in diameter from 30 to 1400 Angstrom units (A) and in their concentration from 10^{16} per gram of silver iodide at temperatures of $-20°c$ to $10^{12.7}$ per gram at $-10°c$. Solution burners based on the above principle have proved to be more efficient

Silver iodide particles, because their crystal structure closely resembles that of ice, provide good nuclei for artificial ice formation. Photograph shows ice crystals, precipitated by silver iodide from a cloud of supercooled water droplets in a laboratory cold box, dropping into a shallow tray of supercooled sugar solution for counting and measuring.

than the solid-fuel burner, a type devised by Vonnegut in the early 1950s. In this latter type, charcoal pellets are soaked in a solution of silver iodide and acetone and then burned to give a smoke of rather impure silver iodide. Whichever type of burner is used the objective is the same: to produce a smoke of potential freezing nuclei that will be carried up into a cloud by natural convection currents. This method of dispersion, so different from that employed for Dry Ice, is the major economic advantage of seeding with silver iodide. Recently, workers in this field have managed to release silver iodide from aircraft, but it has been found that sunlight can reduce the power of the silver iodide to act as a nucleant. Experiments are in hand using various other organic substances, but no definite results have yet been achieved.

Seeding both by Dry Ice and silver iodide depends for its success upon the operation of the Bergeron process. This means that these methods are of little use in clouds whose tops never reach the freezing level, and that if we wish to stimulate precipitation from such clouds, other techniques must be devised. We noted earlier that for coalescence to occur in clouds there must exist some droplets that are comparatively larger than the others in the cloud. These large droplets are probably our only hope of modifying warm clouds. If the number of large droplets in a cloud could be increased, then the collision efficiency of some droplets would also be increased and there would be a greater chance of coalescence and precipitation.

There are two main methods by which large droplets could be induced to develop in clouds. First, large water-attracting nuclei such as salt particles could be fed in near the cloud base. The disadvantage here is that the effects of seeding are very difficult to evaluate: salt nuclei are already present in large numbers in both maritime and continental clouds, so it is difficult to know how many additional nuclei are necessary. Secondly, the obvious, and perhaps at first sight almost ludicrous, way of making large droplets is to spray water into the clouds from aircraft. The idea is that the large droplets introduced into the lower levels of a cloud will rapidly coalesce with the smaller droplets in their passage through the cloud and will eventually grow to raindrop size. It is also possible that some fragmentation of very large drops will occur, setting off a chain reaction. The methods of possible stimulation of precipitation outlined above appear to be quite reasonable from a physical point of view and well worth testing in the field. In fact, ever since the breakthrough in 1947 many tests have been carried out by different authorities. Most of the projects have been undertaken by American and Australian workers, usually with government support, but, particularly in the United States, there has been a good deal of commercial exploitation of possible rainmaking methods. The methods employed in these commercial undertakings are difficult to determine as full reports of the projects are not usually issued: customers pay simply for results, however they are achieved.

Any project designed to test the effectiveness of cloud seeding should be fully randomized to allow as valid an interpretation of the results of the test as possible. This involves establishing a group of clouds that are unseeded as controls and another group that are seeded. Field tests of the mechanism for stimulation or redistribution of precipitation tend to fall into four categories. The first includes an assessment of the influence of seeding on extra-tropical cyclone development; the second is related to migratory cloud systems associated with middle-latitude cyclonic activity; the third to cumulus precipitation; and the fourth to mountain rainfall. This last category is seldom clear-cut as cyclonic and convective factors are often superimposed on the forced lifting. We can see how useful these tests were by considering examples from each category.

One of the earliest and most rigorous tests of the effects of artificial nucleation on cyclone development was Project Scud. This was set up by New York University in the period 1953–54 to find out whether seeding could produce changes in the development stages of cyclone growth, as had been suggested by Langmuir. The project worked on the possibility that "if . . . cyclogenesis is an instability phenomenon, the release of latent heat through seeding might act as a *trigger mechanism* with important consequences for the life history of the storm." Seventeen silver iodide ground generators were used in an area extending from Florida to New York and naval aircraft were used to distribute Dry Ice. Seeding was undertaken in two winters with the silver iodide burners consuming 36 gm/hr. for 12 hours continuously and, in the first winter, each plane dispensing Dry Ice at the rate of 3.2 kg/km. The results of this program suggest that there was no effect on either precipitation or the dynamical development of the treated storms and since this project few, if any, experiments have been performed in any part of the world to test the dynamical effects of seeding such large systems. Many tests have been conducted within such systems but most of them were influenced by the existence of mountains and therefore made it difficult to assess possible influence on cyclogenesis alone. The present scientific basis for predicting the seedability of cyclonic cloud systems over low-land areas is very limited.

Our second category of field test is illustrated by the United States Weather Bureau Artificial Cloud Nucleation Project. This

Cloud-seeding experiment on cumulus clouds in New South Wales. Before seeding, clouds had base at 3300 m., top at 7000 m. and freezing level at 5500 m. Left: nine minutes after 100 kg. of Dry Ice had been dropped into one cloud, radar echoes indicated rain drops and cloud began to rise. Right: 13 minutes after seeding, cloud top rose to 9000 m. and heavy rain started to fall. Far right: cloud eventually formed anvil shape with top between 9000 and 12,000 m.

was concerned with cloud systems within cyclonic storms and was consequently conducted on a smaller scale. The project was undertaken in 1953 and 1954 in western Washington State using only Dry Ice seeding on a randomized basis. Radar and rain gauges provided the data necessary for analysis. The results suggested that there were no significant effects of the seeding.

The modification of cumulus clouds, our third category, perhaps embodies the popular idea of rainmaking in that an individual, white, cauliflower-shaped cloud is made to precipitate by seeding and can be seen to do so. The popular conception is by no means wrong. There are obvious attractions in using an apparently discrete entity in the atmosphere (i.e. an individual cumulus cloud) as an outdoor equivalent of the laboratory cold chamber. Since 1947 many experiments have been undertaken on individual cumulus clouds but none of them has provided the answer to the fundamental problem of whether isolated cumuli constitute promising targets for artificial nucleation because they have comparatively low natural precipitation efficiencies (10 per cent at the most). In fact it has only been possible to formulate this problem with the aid of insight gained from basic research into cloud physics and several major seeding projects.

Basic research, mainly in Australia, the United States, and the United Kingdom, suggests that there are significant differ-

ences between continental and maritime cumuli, perhaps the main difference being that the average droplet radius is twice as great in maritime as in continental clouds. This suggests that the coalescence process would be efficient in maritime cumulus due to the high proportion of initially large droplets; whereas in continental cumuli, coalescence alone would have to operate for a longer time to result in precipitation. These broad statements imply that artificial nucleation in order to create ice crystals would be of little use in maritime cumuli but that there is a possibility that it might stimulate the Bergeron process in continental cumuli with tops at temperatures less than 0°c. Within this framework, much empirical evidence has been gathered by seeding projects.

The earliest cumulus seeding projects were undertaken in Australia and the United States. Australian workers seeded continental cumuli and stratocumuli with airborne silver iodide generators and found that 22 of the 35 seeded gave drizzle or rain. Eight pairs within the total of 35 clouds were chosen so that in each pair, one cloud was seeded and one acted as a control. In only four of the cases did a treated cloud rain and the comparison cloud dissipate. Once again, the importance of randomization of experiment was stressed. In the United States the first of many weather modification experiments took place between December 1949 and June 1951 under the name Project Cirrus. This included seeding of cumulus clouds with ground-based generators and, although some clouds were seen to precipitate, this project provided the first indication of how little we know of the workings of clouds. The most recent test project concerned with modifying cumulus clouds over fairly level terrain was undertaken by the University of Chicago. Project Whitetop, as it was known, was carried out in southern Missouri during the five summers of 1960–64 and included carefully randomized seeding studies as well as measurements of cloud and precipitation parameters. One important way in which Project Whitetop differed from Project Cirrus was that the seeding in Whitetop was done with silver iodide whereas Dry Ice was used in the earlier project. Whitetop used aircraft seeding along a 50-km. arc about 55 km. upwind of a central ground radar site and a rain-gauge network. The data from this project have not yet been fully analyzed, but it appears that there was a significant increase in precipitation in these continental summer cumuli due to silver iodide seeding. Despite these fairly favorable results the workers on the project "note that . . . Whitetop confronts us with many presently unanswerable questions and reveals the rudimentary state of our knowledge of many facets of cloud physics bearing on seeding prospects."

Our fourth category deals with field tests on mountain *(orographic)* cloud systems. Evaluating such tests is extremely difficult simply because the actual effect of mountains upon cloud systems tends to be an unmeasurable factor. The launching of field operations in seeding orographic clouds came somewhat later than those in the first three categories. It was not until 1957 that the Santa Barbara project undertook to seed winter orographic storms and even then the results were suspect because of possible contamination from nearby seeding operations of another project. Similar unprofitable results came from the seeding of summer orographic clouds over the Catalina Mountains in the period 1957–60. No significant differences were found between seeded and unseeded clouds. In Australia five projects have been undertaken over mountainous terrain and none of them produced definitive results. In some cases a decrease in precipitation from seeded clouds was observed, whereas in others the more expected small increase occurred. Despite these inconclusive results both in Australia and the United States, it is the view of many meteorologists that stimulating increased precipitation in certain orographic cloud systems is one of the most promising applications of cloud modification now available.

Hail Modification

We saw in Chapter 1 that heavy falls of hail are hazards to both agriculture and industry. Farmers have suffered the effects of hail on crops for centuries and in the past several methods of hail prevention have been tried out. The earliest records tell us that in Roman times barbarous tribes used to shoot arrows at advancing storms in an attempt to ward them off. In 8th-century Europe church bells were rung at the approach of storms and the 16th century saw the introduction of gunfire as a defense against damaging hail. It was believed that the noise of the bells and guns would scare off the evil spirits in the storms. By the 18th century both bells and guns were well established, but their use was quite often prohibited by law in European countries because of the many disputes between landowners caused by real or supposed effects and because of the alarming rise in the death rate of bell-ringers killed by lightning. At the end of the 19th century, the hail cannon was resurrected in Austria. In 1896 the burgomaster of Windisch-Feistritz set up a network of small cannons in his district and the result was quite dramatic: in the first year of the project there was no hail damage in the area. Despite this success, in 1902 the Austrian government called an international conference on the effects of such cannons and this resulted in their use being soundly condemned.

Although gunfire is now no longer used in attempts to reduce hail damage, and although there was no scientific principle behind its use, it has been superseded by explosive rockets. In the early stage of rocket usage, it was proposed that the shock wave from the explosion would somehow interfere with hailstone growth, resulting in a greater number of smaller stones

Weather modification in the air and on the ground. Left: 50,000 rockets are fired annually in northern Italy, in particular over the Po Valley vineyards, to reduce damage by hail. Right: wind machines are widely used in California's citrus orchards to prevent frost: this is done by mixing warm air above with colder air below.

and thus less damage at the surface. Such ideas fell into disrepute earlier this century, but in the 1950s interest was renewed and several experiments have been undertaken in the past 15 years. Careful analysis of hailstone structure reveals radial fracture lines in the stone, which make it susceptible to shattering, possibly by a shock wave from a rocket explosion. Such results are no doubt heartening to workers in northern Italy where 50,000 rockets are fired annually, mainly over the vulnerable vineyards in the Po valley. More recently an experiment in Kenya, in which rockets, released from sites 500 m. apart, were exploded at either 1500 m. or 2000 m. above ground level, showed a 10 per cent decrease in damage. A second method of hail modification also employs rockets, but in this case the rockets contain silver iodide. The basic idea, as in rainmaking experiments, is to add freezing nuclei to a cloud so as to produce more minute ice particles, and thus promote the growth of more hailstones of a smaller size than would otherwise occur. Some meteorologists think that it is impossible to introduce sufficient nuclei, but as yet the case is not proven and experiments continue. Since 1958 much research effort has gone into studying hailstone growth, but the problem is still far from solved. As recently as July 1967 there was still disagreement as to the nature of the cloud environment in which hailstones are grown. One view is that hail grows in the presence of large concentrations of raindrops suspended aloft; the other view is that it grows in the presence of only modest concentrations of cloud droplets. With so many basic disagreements, it is surprising that so many speculative hail suppression programs have been undertaken.

The most enthusiastic experimenters are working in the USSR. The approach is to try to identify the region in a cloud where hail is beginning to form and then to try to place silver iodide crystals in that region with artillery shells. This method of dispersion of silver iodide contrasts with the more familiar use of ground generators in projects undertaken in the United States, France, Switzerland, Germany, Argentina, and Africa. All except the last of these attempt to increase the number of hailstones in order to decrease their size: they all also suffer from the disadvantage that we do not know just how much we have to increase the number of freezing nuclei in order to get the desired result.

Lightning Suppression

The lightning hazard tends to be greatest in forest areas where there are frequent thunderstorms, as in much of the western United States and eastern Australia. Lightning is simply the spark discharge between two centers of charge that have been separated within a cloud. Usually, positive charge is found at the top of the cloud and negative charge at the bottom. The detailed mechanisms of charge generation, separation, and dissipation are not fully understood and several theories have been put forward in the last 50 years. All of them are unsatisfactory in one way or another. Recently a new theory has been suggested by two British meteorologists, J. Latham and B. J. Mason. They suggest that temperature gradients in fragments of ice can lead to a separation of charge, the cold end taking positive charge and the warm end negative charge. If this mechanism is applied to the freezing of supercooled (below $0°c$) water droplets onto hailstones, it is found that in freezing, the outer shell of the water droplet takes positive charge and the inner core takes negative charge. As the core is frozen to the hailstone, the latter acquires negative charge and carries this downward through the cloud. The cold, positively-charged splinters are carried to the top of the cloud by the updraft. Similarly, if a cold ice crystal collides with a warmer hailstone, the stone becomes negatively charged and the crystal positively charged.

There have been two major attempts to suppress lightning. First, Project Skyfire of the United States Forest Service worked on the principle that the introduction of silver iodide into the supercooled parts of thunderclouds would increase the number of *corona points*—that is, the number of points giving rise to discharges intermediate between the spark discharge (lightning) and the quiet, nonluminous point discharge. Because corona points encourage corona discharge rather than spark discharge, it was then assumed that the introduction of corona points would therefore increase the leakage current between the charge centers in the clouds, suppressing the formation of the first branch of a lightning flash. In view of the importance of ice in the Latham-Mason charging mechanism, it is not really surprising that the results of this project in Montana in 1961 and 1962 did not show significant reduction in lightning occurrence. The introduction of silver iodide could possibly have some effect if the clouds were seeded at a rate that would lead to the formation of as many as 100 ice crystals per 1 cc. of cloud. In theory, such overseeding would freeze all the supercooled water and the electrification process would be modified. Such a project has not been undertaken.

The second project hoped to reduce lightning discharge to corona discharge by dispersing *chaff dipoles* (usually strips of tinfoil with two equal and opposite electric charges at opposite ends) into the thunder cloud. Such experiments, while comparatively easy to formulate, have proved difficult to evaluate but initial tests do suggest that corona activity did result from the introduction of many chaff dipoles.

Our understanding of the lightning mechanism still appears insufficient for us to assess the value of these two methods. Research into cloud electrification has not been lacking in the past decade but it has tended to present workers with more problems than they originally set out to solve. Only when an acceptable theory of cloud electrification has been developed will we be able to assess the possible electrical effects of seeding.

Fogs and Stratus Clouds

In contrast to projects concerned with cumulus clouds, modification of stable cloud layers and of fogs usually means their dissipation. This is particularly true of fog, which, as we saw in Chapter 1, constitutes a great hazard to most forms of transport. The dissipation of supercooled fogs or clouds can sometimes, however, be achieved by the same basic method as the stimulation of rainfall. The cloud or fog is seeded with Dry Ice or silver iodide and ice crystals grow at the expense of water drops until, when the crystals are too large for the updraft to support, they fall out.

This method of dissipating supercooled clouds was tested in the Artificial Cloud Nucleation Project of 1953–55 by the United States Army Signal Corps. This project showed that dissipation took 15 to 50 minutes for breakup to be completed, depending on cloud thickness. Increased snowfall, or rainfall, at the surface occurred on only a minority of occasions: usually the precipitation evaporated before it reached the ground. The reasons for this lie in the thickness of, and vertical motion within, the cloud. In fogs and stratus clouds both characteristics have low values and consequently the effects of seeding are not diffused widely and such particles as are formed have little opposition in their downward fall. In view of the success in clearing supercooled fogs, it is surprising that operational development, particularly at airfields, has not been undertaken on any large scale except in the USSR. This latter routine has been going on since the late 1950s but it was only in the early 1960s that the United States started to put cloud dissipation on an operational footing.

In complete contrast to supercooled clouds, warm clouds and fogs are very difficult to dissipate because they are thermodynamically stable. This is all the more unfortunate because warm fogs occur far more frequently than supercooled fogs. But this high frequency has meant that much effort has gone into devising methods of getting rid of warm fogs and clouds.

One of the earliest and perhaps most reliable ways of dissipating warm fogs is to create a massive heat input by means of oil burners to evaporate the droplets. This was the method employed in the Fog Investigation Dispersal Operations (FIDO) in the United Kingdom in World War II, and there was no doubt that it was successful. Unfortunately, it is a very expensive method of dispersal as it uses large quantities of oil in the burners. An improvement on this idea is the French *Turboclair* technique now being tested on airport runways. This process uses the heat and kinetic energy of obsolete jet engines to vaporize fog droplets. The blast of hot air is directed along the ground in front of the landing strips; it mixes with the surrounding air and lifts the fog near the end of the runway. It has proved remarkably successful and research is continuing in this field. A different approach is the use of large fans to stir the air, thus mixing saturated and unsaturated air. This has the effect of preventing the gentle settling and cooling of air which gives rise to radiation fogs (and frost).

Although some workers have tried to improve the efficiency of this method others have concentrated on completely different approaches. The Japanese have tried seeding warm fogs with water in the hope that the coalescence mechanism would operate, but the clearance that resulted was only temporary. An indirect form of heating aimed at evaporating fog was behind the idea of seeding fogs with carbon black. It was hoped that the carbon black would absorb radiation and calculations based on the assumption of seeding 40 kg. of carbon black per km^2 gave a time of 10 minutes for the evaporation of cloud droplets. Finally, a method suggested and partially tested as early as 1938 is to remove water vapor from foggy air, in this way causing the fog droplets to evaporate. It was suggested that the removal of the water vapor could be achieved by the introduction of calcium chloride, a highly hygroscopic substance, in two ways. First, a highly concentrated solution of calcium chloride could be sprayed into the fog, taking care that the drop size is not so small that they remain suspended, thus adding to the fog. Secondly, calcium chloride powder could be used to dehumidify large volumes of air, which would then be mixed with the fog. In fact, only the first method was tried in the field and it did prove successful. In view of this, it is perhaps surprising that this early work has not been followed up, particularly because of the potential economic benefits to be derived from a successful warm fog clearance routine.

Hurricanes and Tornadoes

The possible methods whereby we could modify cloud dynamics again depend on the introduction of artificial nuclei into a cloud. This is because the only way we can hope to have any effect on the cloud motions is by somehow altering the rate of release of latent heat in the cloud. This release can occur in two ways: either by condensation of vapor, or by the freezing of water. From the point of view of modification, only the latter is worth interfering with, because the amount of supersaturation of water vapor in natural clouds is only of the order of a few per cent. On the other hand, the frequent occurrence of large quantities of supercooled drops in natural clouds provides a

Fogs at temperatures above 0°C can only be cleared if sufficient heat is applied to vaporize the droplets in suspension. In France, the Turboclair process, which uses turbojet engines to generate quantities of air at about 700°C, has proved cheap and successful. Photographs show typical improvement in visibility at 200 m. achieved after a few minutes: the row of turbojets, placed underground is just visible at right of rails in right-hand picture.

great source of latent heat that can be released if the drops can be made to freeze. The familiar seeding by Dry Ice or silver iodide provides the necessary freezing nuclei. Induced freezing releases latent heat of fusion and increases cloud buoyancy: if the release of latent heat is controlled, there is a strong possibility that buoyancy could also be controlled. This would appear to give us a powerful tool in our tinkerings with cloud dynamics. Rigorous tests of these ideas are incorporated in the massive Project Stormfury conducted by the Atmospheric Physics and Chemistry Laboratory of ESSA. This project is still in operation and so any summary of its method and results is, of necessity, incomplete. It is however worthwhile outlining some of its operations because it has a slightly different approach to the modification problem from that of earlier projects. In the Stormfury program, there is at present no effort being directed toward operational weather modification but much useful information is being gathered in the controlled experiments.

The main atmospheric phenomena subject to investigation in Stormfury are individual cumulus clouds and hurricanes. In the cumulus studies, the Stormfury project has the great advantage that a completely quantitative numerical cumulus cloud model exists to predict and compare with the experimental results. The actual operations of Stormfury are once again the seeding of individual cumulus clouds on a random basis. The seeding is done by silver iodide pyrotechnic generators called Alecto units developed by the United States Naval Ordnance Test Station. Data are gathered by five instrumented aircraft, which fly through the clouds at five different levels once before and several times after the seeding run.

In the 1965 cumulus-seeding experiment undertaken in the eastern Caribbean, 22 clouds were investigated; most seeded clouds showed large vertical growth, but the speed of the growth varied. This leads us to the fundamental question: "Under exactly what conditions does seeding do what to cumulus dynamics and physics?" The future of storm modification depends upon an answer that gives the fullest possible specification of conditions. Most meteorologists no longer think that by sprinkling artificial nucleants into a cloud they have solved the weather modification problem. After 20 years of exploratory work, they are now in a position to set up well-designed and controlled experiments having a high information potential, not only for cloud seeding but also for cloud physics generally. The results of Stormfury cumulus studies to date do not appear spectacular but they do provide important first steps in the analysis of cloud dynamics. The project has shown that vertical cloud growth can be enhanced by artificial nucleation in certain specifiable conditions. A cumulus model has been evolved that predicts heights and buoyancies of seeded and un-seeded tropical clouds very well and this implies a strong control on growth by the environmental temperature and moisture structure.

The other major objective of Stormfury is to try to understand hurricane behavior with a view to modifying it. This is perhaps the most ambitious of man's actual, as opposed to hypothesized, attempts to alter the natural development of the weather. As such, it is very much in its infancy.

Although we know very little about hurricanes and their behavior, it is known that the magnitudes of energy transfers and conversions in their working are very high. This fact alone means that any interference with the hurricane mechanism must be either on a massive scale or so carefully undertaken that it triggers some internal instability without great expenditure of materials and efforts. Most of the Stormfury work has

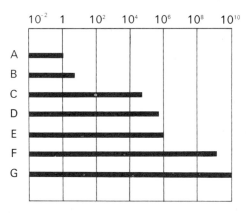

Difficulty in modifying weather systems lies in their sheer magnitude; all but the smallest involve more energy than the largest amounts available to man from thermonuclear weapons. Diagram shows relative total energies, in tons of TNT, of lightning flash (A), waterspout (B), tornado funnel (C), thunderstorm tower (D), megaton thermonuclear bomb (E), moderate Atlantic hurricane (F), and large Atlantic depression (G).

Climate modification on a small scale is illustrated by these wind breaks in Algeria. Wind damage below tornado or hurricane force can be reduced by such tall hedges, which also have beneficial effects upon temperature and humidity.

been directed toward assessing the possibilities of both approaches as well as adding to our knowledge of natural hurricane processes.

Because the problem is so great, and the natural fluctuations in the storms so large that it is difficult to evaluate effects of modification, the actual procedure has followed the same path as all previous projects; that is, seeding. However, the seeding is undertaken in the context of a physically reasonable hypothesis. Early in the project it was suggested that it may be possible to reduce wind speeds in hurricanes by artificial nucleation. It was argued that the added heat of fusion due to seeding would alter the pressure field, leading to an imbalance of forces that, in righting itself, would give a reduction in wind speed and an outward movement of the wall of cloud around the hurricane eye. The results of the first two seedings in 1961 and 1963 appeared to support the hypothesis, but, as mentioned above, the great natural variation in wind speed and cloud behavior means that these results are far from conclusive. The research is continuing.

The final weather system to be considered in this section on cloud modification is the tornado. No experiments have yet been carried out on tornadoes, and there are two main reasons for this. This first reason, again, is lack of knowledge—we simply do not know enough about the dynamics of tornadoes to begin tampering with them. Secondly, although a tornado funnel is thought to have only 10 per cent of the energy exchange of a thunderstorm cell, it is still of such a magnitude as to be far beyond direct control. It is only when an instability point is found in the development of tornadoes that we shall be able to start modifying their behavior. In view of the tremendous amount of damage done by these systems, there is little doubt that any research into their working will be well worth the effort.

Modification of Climate

By far the greater part of this chapter has been devoted to experiments into cloud modification. There are two reasons for this: the heavy concentration on cloud seeding in weather modification experiments; and, as we have stressed throughout this book, the fact that in the opinion of both meteorologist and layman clouds *are* weather. But even though results from cloud modification are only mildly encouraging, the idea of altering the climate of both large and small areas has already come to the minds of many meteorologists. It is argued that if we can interfere with the internal workings of weather systems, it may also be possible to interfere with the basic climatic controls that ultimately govern the initiation, development, and frequency of those systems. This is the logical conclusion of the whole concept of weather modification and, although very few experiments have been undertaken, it is worth ending this chapter by outlining the possibilities.

The most speculative ideas are those that consider alteration of the general circulation of the atmosphere. There is now a wealth of evidence to show that variations in the general circulation must have caused the glacial periods and associated minor climatic fluctuations. If these variations could be controlled, then true control of climate would become a reality. It is not difficult to appreciate that the general circulation governs climate, but this in itself can lead to the postulation of some rather improbable ways of altering the climate. For instance, it has been suggested that the Northern Hemisphere climate could be made milder if the Greenland ice cap were melted by spreading a layer of black, and therefore heat-absorbent, coal dust all over it. Although this cannot be disproved, it would be a most irresponsible undertaking as we have no way of assessing in advance what repercussions it might have on other parts of the atmosphere even if the experiment itself were successful. It is vital therefore that we have a tenable theory of the general circulation before any rash attempts are made to alter its workings. A great deal of research effort, both by laboratory and numerical simulation, has gone and is continuing to go into general circulation studies, but we are still a long way short of an understanding sufficient to allow controlled economic modification.

Compared to the general circulation problem, modification of local climatic characteristics would appear to be simple. In fact, it retains a high degree of difficulty through the complexity of the basic controlling mechanism—the energy budget at the earth's surface. This is of course relevant to the general circulation but in that context it forms only part of a much larger problem. The component parts of the budget are governed by many parameters, the most important being the heat-reflective power of the earth's surface and the composition of the atmosphere itself. One authority gives the number of parameters necessary for complete description of the processes in the budget as 12. Numerical studies of these energy exchanges are only just beginning.

Although we cannot at present fully simulate the energy balance at the earth–atmosphere interface, we do know enough to modify certain elements of local climate. Most of the modification operations are concerned with either temperature or precipitation, depending on the relative importance of each element to human affairs in the area. In midlatitudes, low temperatures provide a hazard that, on a small scale, is capable of being overcome. Frosts can be prevented by the familiar oil burners or giant fans, but the effect is usually only temporary and success can be expected only in a light frost or on the fringe of an area of heavy frost. Wind damage, unless of hurricane or tornado force, can be reduced somewhat by the careful planting of shelter belts. These also have subsidiary beneficial effects on temperature and humidity.

In the arid regions of the world, rainmaking is naturally at a premium. However, the seeding of clouds is not a possible solution in these areas for the simple reason that, for the greater part of the year, clouds do not exist. Once more we must turn to more fundamental causal mechanisms. In fact, a modification program not only has to produce precipitation but it has to produce the clouds as well. This latter requirement is not as ludicrous as it may at first appear. The chief reason for deserts is not a lack of water vapor but a lack of a moisture release mechanism in the atmosphere. The simplest release mechanism is uplift of air: if this could be induced, then cloud, and possibly rainfall, could be made to form. This was shown to be the case in an airstream flowing over an island: the surface heating of the island produced an airflow pattern similar to that known to exist when the wind crosses a mountain range. This is known as the "thermal mountain" effect. Working on this principle it has been suggested that the thermal mountain effect could be achieved by spreading an asphalt coating over desert area, particularly near coasts, in the hope of increasing precipitation downstream. At present this idea is still being tested; we await the results with interest.

The reader will have noted that there has been no description of project techniques in the last section: this is because no projects of this kind have been undertaken. The modification of local and world climate is still very much in the future and it seems more worthwhile to consider what has been and is being done rather than to indicate briefly what it would be nice to do. In describing cloud modification we considered only the experimental work—most of it carried out by government agencies— because operational work is motivated by business interests rather than a desire to understand the true potential of weather modification. Modification is now achieving some kind of respectability in the science of meteorology. Encouraged by this new status, many meteorologists are formulating problems and projects for the future. Some of these are outlined in the next chapter.

6 Prospect

Our look into the future is organized in the same way as the book so far. We start by considering the future plans for observing the weather, as this is basic to the whole subject. It is in this field that the recent planning of the World Meteorological Organization is paramount. This planning culminated in April 1967 with a blueprint for World Weather Watch. We shall consider this in some detail later, and follow it by a brief look at the possibilities of development in analytical techniques. The remainder of the chapter is devoted to research into forecasting and weather modification, and as such takes us to the speculative frontier of meteorology.

Observation

There is little doubt that meteorology is gradually becoming an exact science. We have seen how computers have made it possible to apply the methods of mathematical physics to meteorological analysis, although one result of this has been to show that our description of the atmosphere is still far from

Launching a constant-altitude weather balloon in New Zealand as part of Project GHOST (described in this chapter). New strong plastic films, microminiaturization in electronics, and the advent of earth satellites for relaying information make this method of observation increasingly attractive.

complete. This is brought forcefully to our attention when we try to give an initial state to a numerical model calculation; not only are the data inadequate but the system of communication at present in operation around the world is barely fast enough to keep up with global weather changes. As we have seen, the speedy transmission of comprehensive data of the right kind is vital to successful forecasting. This need has been recognized for some time but only in the 1960s has it proved possible to try to do something about it.

It was perhaps the first satellite pictures that triggered the idea of a world view of the weather. The possibilities of the idea were investigated at length by the advisory committees of the World Meteorological Organization and, in view of the actual and potential developments in satellites, computers, automatic weather stations, and telecommunication techniques, it was decided to plan a World Weather Watch (WWW) to be put into operation between 1968 and 1971. There were three phases in the development of the WWW. First, the broad outlines were put forward in mid-1965; secondly, by mid-1966, a world plan in more or less complete form was prepared; thirdly, the whole plan in full detail was finalized at the Fifth World Meteorological Congress held in Geneva in April 1967. The amount of planning that has gone into this project can be assessed from the fact that 80 studies and surveys were put before the Congress and published as a series of World Weather Watch Planning Reports.

The WWW has five main objectives. Three of them are directly related to the 1968–71 program and the other two embrace longer-term changes. The first three are summarized as follows: a Global Observational System (GOS); a Global Telecommunications System (GTS); and an organization of meteorological centers of various kinds. Longer-term plans include the Global Atmospheric Research Program (GARP) and an international training program.

The heart of the WWW is embodied in GOS. Studies have revealed that observations at ground level are required from an additional 270 stations and that there are 1411 established stations at which the observation program is incomplete. To

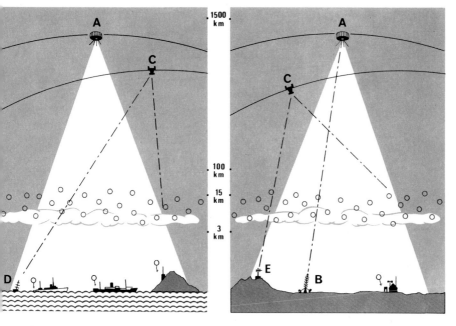

Existing and planned routine observation systems over sea and land. Camera satellites (A) will provide photographs taken at regular intervals and transmitted to land-based receivers (B). Thousands of upper-air balloons (blue), similar to those in GHOST, will drift around the globe at a height of 15–30 km., probably relaying information to interrogator satellites (C) that pass on information from them, and automatic stations (D), to land-based receivers (E).

help fill these gaps, particularly in the Southern Hemisphere, more than 100 ships will be equipped with surface and upper-air instruments and about 40 new land stations and seven new weather ships around Antarctica are planned (see map on pages 172–73). The number of new personnel needed to implement these plans is estimated at 2755. It is hoped to supplement these observations with satellite information, special aircraft reconnaissance flights, meteorological rockets, constant-altitude balloons, and data from automatic weather stations. As the last two are still at experimental stage and are potentially so useful in GOS, it is worth reviewing their capabilities.

The use of constant-altitude balloons is well illustrated in the example of Project GHOST, a joint effort by the United States and New Zealand. GHOST makes use of three important technological advances: the invention of new, strong plastic films; microminiaturization in electronics; and earth satellites.

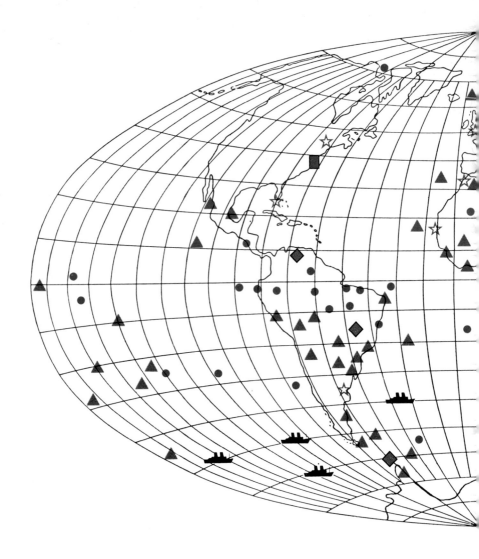

This map shows the additions to the
WMO observation network and the
new world regional communication
and analysis centers planned for the
current World Weather Watch. It is
hoped that all these improvements will
be fully operational by 1971.

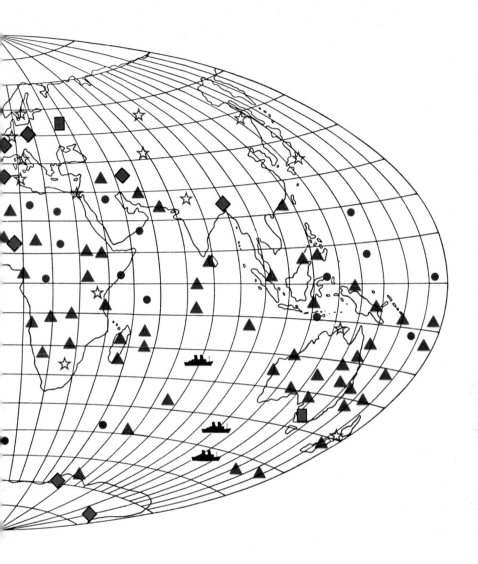

■	World meteorological centers	▲	Upper-air observation stations to be up-graded
☆	Regional meteorological centers	●	Proposed new upper-air stations to be established
◆	Regional telecommunication centers not included in the above categories	🚢	Proposed new fixed-ship ocean weather stations

The idea is to float a balloon with an instrument package at a constant altitude and, by satellite or ground interrogation, establish the temperature, humidity, and wind speed at that altitude at various locations around the globe. At present, it is an experimental project and so all interrogation is from the ground.

The theoretical capabilities of balloons made to fly at different altitudes are summarized in the diagram opposite. The initial test program was to fly 100 balloons at 500, 200, and 30 mb., and the first launching took place in March 1966. The balloons are tracked by stations in New Zealand, French Polynesia, Peru, Brazil, Argentina, Zambia, Angola, South Africa, Mauritius, and Australia. So far, despite icing and leakage troubles, the project is proving a success. One of the balloons, launched in the spring of 1966, had circled the earth 16 times by October and was still in good condition. The information it had provided by that date was roughly equivalent to 100 upper-air soundings, distributed uniformly over the Southern Hemisphere, but at far less cost. It is hoped eventually to have 5000 such balloons circling the earth at heights from 3000 m. to 25,000 m., interrogated by three satellites at the same altitude around the equator. The potentialities of this project are well summarized in the words of its director: "If all expectations are met, we shall be able to furnish a suitably programed computer with a complete and continual description of the physical state of the atmosphere on a global basis. With such data we hope to be able to provide useful predictions of the atmospheric circulation."

Automatic stations are of two kinds. First, there are the stations that themselves transmit automatically the values of meteorological measurements that they carry out. Secondly, there are the climatological stations, which merely record the values. Both are interesting, but the first is the type that will be of most use to forecasters and is therefore considered here.

Five components go to make an automatic transmitting weather station. They are the sensors, the coding devices, the transmitters, the programming unit, and the power supply unit. The number of sensors on any particular station varies, but

Theoretical lives of various balloons in GHOST test program. Figures at top are (A) balloon diameter in meters and (B) film thickness in microns. Bigger balloons last longer simply because gas diffuses more slowly from balloons of large diameter for given film thickness.

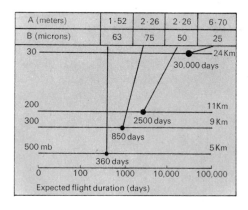

A (meters)		1·52	2·26	2·26	6·70
B (microns)		63	75	50	25

usually pressure, temperature, wind speed and direction, and precipitation are measured. Relative humidity measurements suffer from many sources of error and have caused many headaches in station design. Coding systems were initially of the same type as used in radiosondes, but for technical and economic reasons they now work on a chronometer principle where the value of any element is a function of the time taken between pulses from successive electrical contacts geared to the appropriate sensor. Radio is generally used for transmission and the control of the operation is done by the programming unit of the station. For a completely isolated station using radio, the programming unit has to control the following operations: the warming-up period for the transmitters; the period in which the station call sign is transmitted; the "reading" of the various instruments; the transmission of the measurements; the possible resetting to zero of various instruments; and the automatic switching-off of the station. All these depend ultimately on the power unit for their completion. At isolated stations the power may be provided by batteries, although solar and atomic energy models have already been designed.

The workings of an automatic weather station have been presented in some detail so that the difficulties of automatic monitoring may be appreciated. The rarity of such stations after 20 years' experimentation is a testimony to the technical difficulties that have been met. One of the largest stumbling blocks has been the collection of reports from remote locations quickly enough for them to be of operational use. It is hoped that once again satellites will provide the solution, by being able to interrogate these remote stations when in radio contact. This is closely linked to the GHOST project idea and the Interrogation, Recording, and Location System (IRLS), including both balloons and automatic weather stations (on land and sea), was scheduled for early 1968. A further benefit from the GHOST project is the development of an automatic weather station using electronics. It is called MOSES and is of simple design, costs less than $1000 exclusive of sensors, and is capable of operation in any environment except polar. It is hoped that eight observations a day will be possible by interrogation.

We can now turn to the second major objective of the WWW —the Global Telecommunications System (GTS). We saw in Chapter 3 that one of the weakest links in weather analysis for forecasting was the comparative slowness of the present communications system. The planned increase in data from GOS makes a more efficient system of communications essential. The GTS will meet this need by collecting and transmitting raw data from and to meteorological centers and by distributing prepared analyses and forecasts in digital or pictorial form. The new system will have a Main Trunk Circuit as its base, operating at a speed of 3600 words a minute, or 50 times faster than a teleprinter.

The Main Trunk Circuit links the three World Meteorological Centers, which form the basis of the third major part of the WWW. The centers, already in operation, are in Washington, Moscow, and Melbourne. These centers will be linked with Regional and National Meteorological Centers and Regional Telecommunication Centers. The function of the World Meteorological Centers will be to prepare pictures of global weather twice a day. They will also relay any appropriate material to other world, regional, or national centers and prepare prognoses once or twice daily. The Regional Meteorological Centers will provide a link between the World and National Centers. They will also have large computers to receive, check, store, and analyze data and their analyses and

Anchoring an automatic weather station in mid-ocean. Unmanned observation platforms like this one carry sensors, coding devices, transmitters, programming unit, and power supply; the one in the picture is powered by the small windmills in the foreground.

forecasts will be available to the countries served by the centers. As they will have access to the Main Trunk Line, it is possible that data will be passed from automatic weather station, to satellite, to World Meteorological Center, to Regional and even National Center without being "touched by human hand."

The three-part organization of the WWW opens up tremendous opportunities for improvement of routine forecasts, both in content and in length. In addition, it will give the first glimmerings of a picture of world weather, something that has never before been achieved. It is in the light of this that the Global Atmospheric Research Project has been suggested. This will build on the results of the WWW and consolidate research into

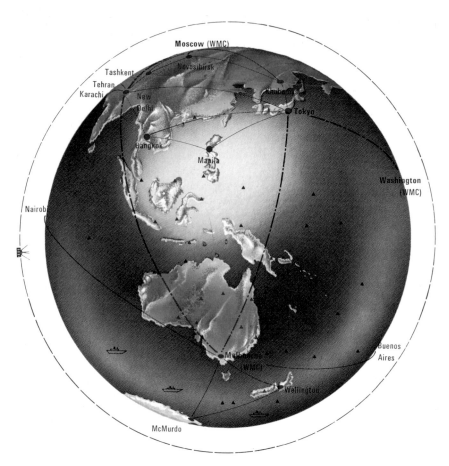

Proposed telecommunications links of the World Weather Watch over the Pacific area. Thick broken line represents Main Trunk Circuit; unbroken lines the regional circuits; triangles are new or up-graded upper-air stations and ships, and outer circle represents existing satellite coverage.

weather patterns in the Arctic and Antarctic regions, the movement of air masses in the tropics, the relationships between weather phenomena in the Northern and Southern Hemisphere, and the interaction between ocean and atmosphere. Once again, this project will require the cooperation of about 100 countries.

The final and most important part of the general concept of the WWW is the training of meteorologists and the supplying of technical assistance to countries that cannot meet their own requirements. In the wealthier countries, it is hoped to establish university fellowships and scholarships to attract scientists to meteorology. On an international level, the World Meteorological Organization has proposed the initiation of a Voluntary Assistance Program to which member countries could contribute money, equipment, and services according to their various abilities. It is hoped to get this under way in the period 1968–71.

Analysis

In considering the future of weather observation, it was possible to give a summary of definite plans. This is far more difficult in the case of analytical techniques. It is the objects of analysis that change rather than the techniques themselves. There are many plans for studies of various atmospheric phenomena on all scales, but the methods of analysis, although dependent to some extent on observations, are basically those outlined in Chapter 3. It would be possible to give a long list of future analyses but it is perhaps more important to pick out those to which priority has been given by the various national meteorological centers. This brief summary is concerned with research rather than routine.

A tremendous amount of work is going into the numerical simulation of the general circulation of the atmosphere. A major contribution is a nine-level model of the atmosphere, including condensation processes, which has recently been integrated for 187 days on a hemispherical basis. This was remarkably successful, for not only was the mean hemispheric rate of precipitation reproduced, but the distribution of relative humidity in the troposphere and stratosphere was in qualitative agreement with observation and the momentum and heat budgets were nearer reality than in a dry model; nevertheless it is hoped to improve even further on this wet model. Plans for future research include the use of grids with a smaller mesh, better ways of computing radiative transfer, and the use of global integrations instead of hemispheric ones to get a more realistic picture.

This is only one indication of the direction in which weather analysis is moving, but national meteorological center reports

Left: single frame from a numerically produced forecast of surface pressure distribution. A Control Data 6600 system (opposite) at National Center for Atmospheric Research, Boulder, Colorado, uses a six-level baroclinic model to simulate continuous pressure patterns; the equations are advanced in steps corresponding to five minutes of real time. Results are displayed on cathode-ray tube, recorded on microfilm, and then projected faster to give time-lapse representation of systems.

outline many other subjects that await analysis—ranging from the upper atmosphere and the polar atmosphere, through hurricanes and severe local storms, to turbulence and diffusion studies. Indeed the scope is enormous and it is only with increased automation that any real progress will be made. The potentialities of objective analysis by automated methods are signposted by an example of what computers are able to do at present. At the National Center for Atmospheric Research in Boulder, Colorado, a computer produces weather maps from mathematical models of the general circulation and displays the output on a cathode-ray tube. Individual weather maps are computed at successive intervals of time and each chart is photographed by a 35-mm. camera controlled by the computer. The resulting sequence of frames is then projected at a faster speed to give a time-lapse representation of the evolution of the computed weather patterns, showing the growth, movement, and decay of weather systems on a global scale. Such capability in the handling of data promises well for future analysis and forecasting. Indeed, future developments in forecasting are heavily dependent on the parallel developments in numerical analysis, and make separate treatment of the two techniques somewhat artificial.

Forecasting

Assessment of future developments in forecasting technique is beset by the same difficulties we met in our brief consideration of analysis. Today's research is tomorrow's routine, and this research is being conducted into such a wide range of subjects that it is impossible to review them all. This section is therefore concerned with a selection of projects that will probably be of use to future forecasters.

In the familiar realm of synoptic forecasting, there will continue to be many small contributions aimed at increasing the usefulness of any given technique. This is particularly true of the synoptic fine structure such as fog, local temperatures, and diurnal fluctuations. The suggested improvements are often the result of empirical studies but there are examples of a more fundamental approach. For instance, studies are being undertaken to develop a dynamical model that will predict sea-level pressure for up to 18 hours ahead. Other examples include physical modeling of warm-front and radiation fogs. This type of research into forecasting technique can often be easily phased into improvements of forecasts for specific purposes such as agricultural, marine, and forest-fire operations.

Important as these developments are, it is probable that the greater part of future work on forecasting will be directed toward improving the quality of numerical predictions. Any improvement requires not only a better forecasting technique, but more data for the calculations and a parallel advance in computer technology. It is hoped that the WWW will go some way toward providing the required data; the main problem in computation is that no sooner is one machine operational than a bigger and better one is designed. Economics plays nearly as great a role as technology itself. But economics apart, the fact that we now have computers on the market that are 10 times more powerful than the largest and fastest used today in numerical weather prediction gives rise to a cautious optimism about what will be available in the near future.

Research into numerical weather prediction will probably concentrate on two main aspects—the improvement of atmospheric models for large-scale circulations with a view to extending the useful forecast period, and the construction of models for circulations on the synoptic scale or less to increase the amount of detail in a forecast. The two branches are, of course, mutually beneficial.

In Chapter 4 we saw how the majority of large-scale models in operational numerical prediction use the modified hydrodynamical equations for two levels. Future developments will concentrate on improving the capabilities of the baroclinic primitive equation model. Two major problems present themselves. First, it is necessary to include the effects of large-scale air flow over mountains, friction between the air and the surface of the earth, and heating or cooling of the atmosphere at the earth's surface in future models. This has been done by some national meteorological centers but there is always room for improvement, so that detail in 2–3 day forecasts is more fully described. The second major problem is the inclusion in a prediction model of the atmospheric sources and sinks of heat due to the changes of phase of water. Release of latent heat gives rise to high vertical velocities and the numerical simulation of this process tends to run into mathematical instabilities. There is no doubt that much research effort will go into attempts to solve this problem.

On a smaller scale than these models are those that predict atmospheric behavior on the synoptic scale. In this context, frontal zones are particularly important. The major problem is simply one of scale. Fronts are of such dimensions that the routine aerological network is too coarse to give an adequate description of frontal structure as a basis for a forecast. A second problem resulting from the characteristic dimensions of frontal zones is that the quasi-geostrophic approximations of the dynamical equations often used in large-scale models become increasingly invalid when applied to systems with a scale less than 1000 km. Because ageostrophic motions are important near fronts, it is necessary to use the primitive equations in any model set up to simulate frontal conditions.

One such model has recently been tested. It was a 10-level primitive equation model in which the atmosphere was considered to be hydrostatic and inviscid and the effects of friction and topography were ignored. However, the effects of latent heat were included up to the 300-mb. level, above which the atmosphere was considered to be dry. A further important characteristic of this experiment was the horizontal grid length of 40 km.—far smaller than the lengths usually employed in numerical prediction. This initial test was successful in that for a 24-hour period it forecast vertical velocities that could account for the observed mesoscale rainfall distribution in a frontal zone. It is hoped that the introduction of topographic effects and better specification of boundary conditions will improve on the present performance. The implementation of these plans will take several hours on the fastest computers now available, but there is little doubt that this scale of numerical prediction will become operational in the not-too-distant future.

Modification

In Chapter 5 it was suggested that conscious modification of the basic climatic factors was still some way off, and that the reasons for this lie in the inadequacy of our present knowledge and simulation of the general circulation and the limited energy at our command. Two further types of observation are badly needed to construct a model that would be useful for modification. Both of them are measurements of boundary-layer processes. First, we need to measure the boundary fluxes of mass, momentum, and energy; and this will require special, nonroutine observational equipment. Secondly, we need to measure the predominantly horizontal transfer processes throughout the depth of the boundary layer; and this again requires special equipment. Although these are not strictly future developments in modification, they are vital steps toward changing the general circulation. Enough has been said throughout this book for the reader to realize that it is virtually impossible to have a master plan for general circulation studies. It is by the accumulation of many studies based on both observation and theory that advances will be made.

On a more substantial footing, it is possible to give some idea of probable developments in cloud-seeding and associated procedures. It is highly likely that, for some time yet, weather modification will be restricted to cloud nucleation. Within the field, three major problems and prospects present themselves: the evaluation of cloud-seeding effects; developments in instruments and techniques in cloud-modification research; and research into the atmospheric water budget.

The shortcomings of present methods of evaluation of cloud-seeding effects have caused much heart-searching among meteorologists engaged in this work. No definitive and quantitative conclusion even about the effectiveness of silver iodide has been reached, and it is thought that careful statistical manipulation in future may go some way toward strengthening evaluations. Few definite plans have been made but it is possible to outline some suggestions as to what could be done.

Due to the great natural fluctuations in the atmosphere and the comparatively limited amount of cloud-seeding data available, it is envisaged that a simple increase in data as a result of enlargement in both time and space of the test projects would give a more representative statistical population than the one we have at present. This has proved to be the case in many other subjects and would probably, if it had been done at a far earlier stage in meteorology, have been more economic than the many separate projects outlined in the previous chapter. An

Doppler radar is used to measure movement of rain or snow particles. Position, size, and movement of rightmost pulse on broad green line indicates height, size, and numbers of particles, and their speed up or down. Speed is measured by noting change in echoes, whose frequency varies like pitch of train's whistle as it passes.

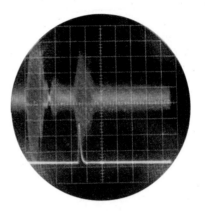

alternative to increasing data of the same kind is the collection of new kinds. In this way there is a distinct possibility that hitherto undiscovered sources of variation in an experiment would be found and their elimination would lead to an increase in the decisiveness of the project.

These possible improvements may appear rather abstract when compared to developments in the actual hardware of cloud seeding. Cloud physics research generally would benefit from better sensors and instrument vehicles for taking measurements of cloud properties. For instance, Doppler radar and lasers have recently shown great potential observational capabilities and no doubt they will be investigated further. In cloud seeding proper, there has recently been much effort put into the testing of various organic materials as cloud seeds, but most of this work has tended to confirm the superiority of Dry Ice and silver iodide. Despite the widespread use of these two agents, there is a surprising ignorance of the actual way in which they work. In the case of Dry Ice, more analyses are needed of the heat transfer and aerodynamics of free-falling pellets. Our knowledge of the processes by which silver iodide works is also far less comprehensive than was first thought.

In spite of these drawbacks, it is highly unlikely that seeding with silver iodide will be abandoned. Although there have been several versions of the silver iodide generator, almost nothing is known in detail about the chemical and physical processes

Meteorologists have already found uses for the versatile laser. Among its applications are the detection and analysis of clouds, dust particles, turbulence, and invisible atmospheric layers. This double-barreled lidar (laser radar) was developed for this purpose by Stanford Research Institute, California.

taking place within them. It is quite possible that the output of these generators could be improved with a more comprehensive knowledge of these internal processes. Moreover, research into the different methods of introducing silver iodide into the clouds is needed so that the most efficient one may be employed. As yet, there has been no rigorous study of the relative advantages of aircraft seeding and ground generator seeding.

Finally, there is the problem of the possible effects of persistence in silver iodide seeding. In the past few years there have been increasing indications in both Australia and the United States that silver iodide somehow persists in a target area and produces a delayed seeding effect weeks or even months after release. This may explain why many seedings appeared to lose their potency as a test series went on. Various ideas have been put forward in explanation, particularly by Australian workers, but a full investigation of this phenomenon is badly needed.

The last of our three major requirements in future weather modification programs is a better understanding of the atmospheric water budget. This is in contrast to the more tangible engineering requirements of seeding proper, but is similar to the necessity for careful project design in that it forms one of the foundation stones of all weather modification. To assess the effects of cloud modifications, we require quantitative studies of the *water budget*—where the water comes from, where it goes to, and how it travels in between. This would appear to be an obvious basic necessity to any large-scale modification of precipitation because it would indicate, before any such scheme were undertaken, where the most likely places for natural precipitation would occur. The concept of the water budget is also relevant on many smaller scales. It can be applied to the precipitation efficiency of storm systems and individual clouds, but the fulfillment of the concept must await future elaborate experimentation.

This review of the prospects for weather technology has been brief and inevitably highly selective. Only the most important future developments have been mentioned. In some cases, such as observation, it has been possible to outline definite plans: in others, such as modification, our description consists of research requirements rather than firm plans. This underlines again the wide difference between routine weather analysis and forecasting, which are now rapidly becoming more international in character, and basic research into the atmosphere, which is not. However, it is likely that the present highly national attitude to research will be influenced by the global approach to routine weather analysis represented by the WWW. If this is so, and research is undertaken on a more thorough, worldwide basis, meteorology will have crossed an important threshold in its development. We await the crossing with great interest.

Suggested Reading

L. J. Battan *Cloud Physics and Cloud Seeding,*
Doubleday (New York, 1962) Heinemann (London, 1962)

L. J. Battan *Radar Meteorology,* University of Chicago Press
(Chicago, 1959)

British Meteorological Office *Observer's Handbook, Handbook of
Meteorological Instruments,* and *Weather Map,* Her Majesty's
Stationery Office (London, 1956).

C. L. Godske, T. Bergeron, J. Bjerknes, R. C. Bundgaard
Dynamical Meteorology and Weather Forecasting, American
Meteorological Society and Carnegie Institution of Washington
(Washington D.C., 1957)

R. E, Huschke (Ed.) *Glossary of Meteorology,* American
Meteoroligical Society (1959)

J. Namias *An Introduction to the Study of Air Mass and Isentropic
Analysis,* American Meteorological Society (1940)

National Academy of Sciences—National Research Council *Weather
and Climate Modification: Problems and Prospects,* Vols. I and II
(Washington. D.C., 1966)

S. Petterssen *Weather Analysis and Forecasting,* Vols. I and II,
McGraw-Hill (New York, 1956)

W. J. Saucier *Principles of Meteorological Analysis,*
University of Chicago Press (Chicago, 1955)

P. D. Thompson, *Numerical Weather Analysis and Prediction,* Collier-
Macmillan (London, 1961)

W. K. Widger (Jr.) *Meteorological Satellites,*
Holt, Rinehart and Winston, Inc. (New York, 1966)

Picture Credits

Page 8 *The Sunday Times Magazine,* photo Colin Simpson: 12 From "Medical-
meteorological forecasting: an application of fundamental bioclimatological concepts,"
by F. Sargent II and D. S. Zeharko; a paper in *Biometeorology,* ed. S. W. Tromp,
Pergamon Press Limited, Oxford, 1962: 16 Photo Blake Allison from the set of color
slides *Storms,* by Diana Wyllie Limited: 17 (Top left) *The Sunday Times Magazine,* photo
Donald McCullin (Top right) Shell International Petroleum Company Limited: 20 By
courtesy of Central Electricity Generating Board: 21 (Top left) Photo W. J. Allen (Top
right) Barnabys/John Dart: 24 NASA photo: 28, 29 Photos from the color filmstrip
Meteorological Instruments, by Diana Wyllie Limited: 32 (Top left) Photo Michael
Holford, (Top right bottom) Photos from the color filmstrip *Meteorological Instruments,*
by Diana Wyllie Limited: 33 (Top left) Photo Michael Holford (Right) Photos from the
color filmstrip *Meteorological Instruments,* by Diana Wyllie Limited: 35, 37 World
Meteorological Office, Geneva: 40 (Top) Diana Wyllie Limited/R. S. Scorer (Bottom
right) From *Journal of Applied Meteorology,* Vol. 2, The American Meteorological

Society, 1963: 42 British Crown copyright, reproduced with the permission of the Controller, Her Britannic Majesty's Stationery Office: 43 (Top left) Philips Rubber Soles Limited, Manchester (Top right) Science Musuem, London, photo Michael Holford: 45 World Meteorological Office, Geneva: 47 From W. K. Widger, Jr., *Meteorological Satellites*. Holt, Rinehart and Winston, Inc., Publishers, New York © 1966: 48 (Bottom left) *Meteorological Magazine*, November 1965 (Bottom right) Bristol Aerojet Limited: 52 NASA photo: 53, 54 (Top) Courtesy ESSA (Bottom) NASA photo: 55 (Bottom) Meteorological Office, Bracknell, photo Michael Holford; reproduced with permission of the Controller, Her Britannic Majesty's Stationery Office: 56 *Life* © Time Inc: 57 From T. Fujita, *Analytical Mesometeorology*, Met. Monog. Vol. 5, No. 27, American Meteorological Society, 1963: 60 Meteorological Office, Bracknell, photo Michael Holford: 63 S. Petterssen, *Weather Analysis and Forecasting*, Vol. II, © 1956, McGraw-Hill Book Company, New York: 64 (Top) From R. C. Sutcliffe, F.R.S., *Weather and Climate*, George Weidenfeld & Nicholson Limited, London, 1967, and W. W. Norton & Company Inc., New York © 1966: 65 Meteorological Office, Bracknell, photo Michael Holford: 68 World Meteorological Office, Geneva: 69 Meteorological Office, Bracknell, (Bottom) photo Geoffrey Drury (Top) photo Michael Holford: 71 From *Meteorological Office Handbook of Weather Forecasting*, Vol. I; British Crown copyright, reproduced with the permission of the Controller, Her Britannic Majesty's Stationery Office: 72 World Meteorological Office, Geneva: 73, 76 (Top) J. S. Sawyer, *Meteorological Analysis—A Challenge for the Future*, Quarterly Journal of Royal Meteorological Society, 1964: 77 (Top) Meteorological Office, Bracknell, photo Michael Holford (Bottom) From J. W. Wilson and E. Kessler III, "Use of radar summary maps for weather analysis and forecasting", *Journal of Applied Meteorology*, Vol. 2, 1963: 78 J. S. Sawyer, *Meteorological Analysis—A Challenge for the Future*, Quarterly Journal of Royal Meteorological Society, 1964: 80 Meteorological Office, Bracknell, photo Geoffrey Drury; reproduced with the permission of the Controller, Her Britannic Majesty's Stationery Office: 85 Meteorological Office, Bracknell, photos Studio Briggs: reproduced with the permission of the Controller, Her Britannic Majesty's Stationery Office: 86 From *Meteorological Office Handbook of Weather Forecasting*, Vol. I; British Crown copyright, reproduced with the permission of the Controller, Her Britannic Majesty's Stationery Office: 90, 91 P. E. Sherr, "Suggested procedures for operationally integrating meteorological satellites and conventional data for extratropical regions", *Journal of Applied Meteorology*, Vol. 5, 1966: 92, 93 Meteorological Office, Bracknell, photos Geoffrey Drury; reproduced with the permission of the Controller, Her Britannic Majesty's Stationery Office: 97 Meteorological Office, Bracknell, photo Studio Briggs; reproduced with the permission of the Controller, Her Britannic Majesty's Stationery Office: 98 Meteorological Office, Bracknell, photo Geoffrey Drury: 100 Courtesy ESSA: 106 H. Riehl, *Introduction to the Atmosphere*, © 1965, McGraw-Hill Book Company, New York: 109 Air Weather Service (MAC), United States Air Force: 110 *Meteorological Magazine*, September 1965: 113 *Meteorological Magazine*, November 1966: 119 L. F. Richardson, *Weather Prediction by Numerical Process*, Dover Books, New York, 1965: 120 Princeton University: 124 G. P. Cressman, "Numerical weather prediction in daily use," *Science* 148, © 1965 by the American Association for the Advancement of Science: 125 Photo Ivan Masser, Black Star, New York: 131 G. P. Cressman, "Numerical weather prediction in daily use," *Science* 148, © 1965 by the American Association for the Advancement of Science: 137 Photo Harrison Forman: 141 By courtesy of Radiophysics Laboratory, C.S.I.R.O.: 145 S. Petterssen, *Weather Analysis and Forecasting*, Vol. II, © 1956, McGraw-Hill Book Company, New York: 146 (Left) Photo Dr. J. D. Woods, Meteorological Office, Bracknell: 148 General Electricity Company, Schenectady: 149, 153 By courtesy of Radiophysics Laboratory, C.S.I.R.O.: 156 (Left) Photo G. Tomsich, Roma (Top right) Photo Prof. H. B. Schultz, University of California, Davis: 161 Photos Bertin & Co. and Paris Airport: 163 *Science Journal*, January 1968: 164 Photo Dr. Georg Gerster, Zurich: 168 National Centre for Atmospheric Research, Boulder: 171 *The Sunday Times Magazine*: 172 World Meteorological Office, Geneva: 175 *Science Journal*, June 1967: 177 Courtesy ESSA: 180, 181 National Centre for Atmospheric Research, Boulder: 185 Photo Ivan Masser, Black Star, New York: 186 United States Information Service, London.

Index Page numbers in *italics* refer to illustrations.